Contents

Acknowledgements

I wish to acknowledge my debt to the late Professor C. L. Mowat of the University College of North Wales, Bangor, for the guidance he gave me with the original M.A. thesis that forms the chief source of material for this book.

I am further indebted to the Librarian of the Liverpool Local History Library and his colleagues for their help with essential research, and Mr. Mike Stammers, Keeper of the Merseyside Maritime Museum, for his most generous advice. For the loan of illustrative material I thank the Trustees of the National Museums and Galleries on Merseyside and the Liverpool Daily Post.

May I also thank Brian Dolan, B.A., Peter Woolley, Tony Mossman, Merseyside police press and publicity officer, John D. Robertson, Jim Gonzales, Mrs. P. Brown, Mrs. Margaret Caulfield, too, who assisted in setting up the manuscript and my wife, Barbara, and family who have been a constant source of encouragement in my endeavours.

William R. Cockcroft
19 Bowness Ave
Ainsdale
Southport PR8 3QP

The Albert Dock
&
Liverpool's Historic
Waterfront

W. R. Cockcroft

Print Origination
Formby, Merseyside

The Albert Dock and Liverpool's Historic Waterfront

W. R. Cockcroft

This book is dedicated to my parents, Emily and Henry Cockcroft

ISBN 0 903348 48 9

Typeset and compiled by Print Origination Formby
and Books Unlimited, Rainworth, NG21 0JE
Printed and bound by Cromwell Press Ltd
Melksham, Wilts.

Preface

In recent years the riverfront of Liverpool has
re-awakened to remind the world of its unique heritage.
Within the Albert Dock complex, settings such as the
restored Pilotage, the Boat Hall, the Piermaster's House,
the Cooperage and the Albert warehouses themselves
have helped to promote the Maritime Museum housed
there as one of the finest at an international level. The
Albert warehouses now also contain attractive shopping
facilities, TV studios, stylish restaurants, luxurious homes
and the remarkable Tate Art Gallery exhibition. These
contrast with the quality of life to be found at or near the
Albert Dock when it opened in 1846. The dock was
designed as a model of security against fire-raising and
pilferage.

 The Albert Dock was one of the most remarkable of those
waterways constructed at the heart of Liverpool's South
Docks. These had essentially been developed to cater for
the needs of a host of different types of sail-powered
ships. Within this waterfront district, rightly regarded as
the domain of a manly breed of international sailors, an
entire way of life catering for the tastes of several
distinctive groups of people came into being.

In time the dock-building navvies, the desperate emigrants and the bold mariners became the vigorous sinews of a volatile community. Into such a community, with its traditional disrespect for law and order, stepped Liverpool's police constables in 1836. This body of peelers, intially modelled and organized by former London police officers, was forced to experience at first hand the harsh and often dangerous realities of patrolling a dockland beat in a world famous international seaport.

 This book has been compiled from a thesis that has already been used to help illustrate some of the desperate aspects of Liverpool city life, from 1836 to 1902. Those parts developed below, however, have essentially remained unpublished and inaccessible to those wishing to read about dockland life, at, or near, the Albert Dock during its prime as a Victorian warehouse centre.

The location of Victorian sites in relation to modern Liverpool

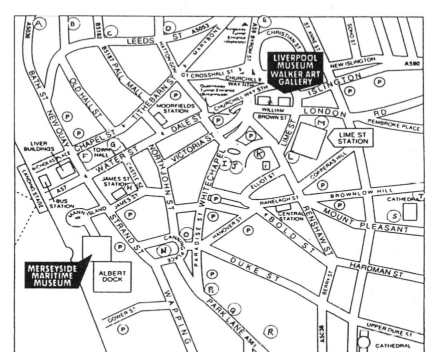

A.   Warehouse fires of 1842 in Neptune and Formby Streets
B.   The Borough Gaol in Great Howard Street.
C.   The beerhouses of Leeds Street.
D.   The Infirmary, Bridewell and beerhouses of Vauxhall Road.
E.   The beerhouses of Scotland Road.
F.   Sailors' quarters in New Quay.
G.   The Exchange at the Town Hall.
H.   The central dock police station in James Street.
I.   The Penny Hop in Hood Street.
J.   The Free Concert Hall in Williamson Square.
K.   The Fun Stalls of Roe Street.
L.   The Hop beerhouse in Lime Street.
M.   The Concert Hall in Lord Nelson Street.
N.   The Custom House of Canning Place.
O.   The Sailors' Home in Canning Place.
Ps.   Sailors' boarding houses in Cleveland Square.
Q.   Sailors' lodgings in Frederick Street.
R.   Concert and gambling halls in Nelson Street.
S.   Cellar dwellings in Duckinfield Street.
T.   The Liverpool workhouse of Brownlow Hill.

1

Life on Liverpool's Victorian Waterfront

Few who visit the Albert Dock warehouses today will doubt that they are among some of the most spectacular remaining examples of British nineteenth century technology. Equally important is the need to remember that the port of Liverpool in the eighteen forties was the goal of countless seafarers and the daily scene of the working lives of many thousands on its waterfront who experienced a quality of life that was generally arduous and fraught with many dangers.

The Albert Dock was constructed within Liverpool's south docks close to the pierheads and the heart of Liverpool. Visitors to the port in the eighteen forties found it to be on the north side of the River Mersey opposite to the Cheshire shore. Each important place on the south side was linked to Liverpool by a steamboat ferry. Travelling by night across the river on one of these paddle-wheeled ferry boats from the chief ferry point, Birkenhead, visitors would have witnessed 'a forest of masts among which lamps and lanterns were glittering like so many glow worms in a grove.'

Vessels in port, including coasters, reputedly about 10,000 at this time were overlooked landward by Liverpool's

Duke's Dock, c 1905
The shipment of foodstuffs dominated the early use of this dock. As the Liverpool industrial hinterland grew so did the demands upon this dock. Its cargoes included sugar, spices, tea and corn. At the adjacent King's Dock grain ships discharged their cargoes into warehouses. Flat boats were then reloaded with the food as they waited in the Duke's Dock. This busy scene reflects the dependence of the Dock on its cranes, transit sheds and barges.

Wapping Dock, Liverpool, c 1909
The famous phrase "a forest of masts" is partly illustrated in this remarkable scene showing the crowded western quayside of the Wapping Dock. Built as a connecting dock, it shows its single-storey transit shed on a quayside fully occupied with sailing and coastal steam vessels.

great buildings including the Custom House, The Exchange, the docks complex and Lime Street railway station. These docklands were spectacularly marked by a commercial bustle made unique by the close proximity of the magnificent buildings to the docks. It became part of Liverpool's reputation that a merchant might almost make himself heard in the docks out of his own countinghouse window. Liverpool's entire length of river frontage, moreover, was filled with its docks.

Crowding into these and their adjoining basins, filled with ships, were dock labourers loading and unloading a vast range of merchandise.

Whenever ships docked they had the added advantage of an unvarying depth of dock water and ideal facilities for effecting repairs. Each class of ship moreover, had a special dock to cater for it. American vessels laden with timber sailed into the Brunswick; West Indian, Baltic and Dutch vessels entered the Queen's Dock; the largest class of sea-going steamers tied up at the Coburg Dock; tobacco vessels from the West Indies and America used the King's Dock; and into the Prince's Dock, the most outstanding when the Albert was built, ships sailed from India and China together with the largest class of American ship. Each of these docks had special features for the type of vessel it was constructed to accommodate. Each dock also had an attached basin so that a vessel could enter it, directly from the Mersey, at every period of the tide.

In the basins the vessels might shelter whilst waiting for

the dock to open, at high tide. Should any dock be found to be in need of enlargement, as the Salthouse Dock in the early forties, relays of labourers would be sent to work in twelve hour shifts both by day and night. Throughout the night as many as 300 navvies might be seen working by torchlight, hacking, digging, breaking up or exploding rock to enlarge it.

Close to the edge of the quays the dock labourers made use of the long sheds, where possible, to shelter the off-loaded merchandise.

Once inside the sheds they then onloaded goods into waggons for carriage out of the docks. Should heavy rain or storms occur the men closed over the wooden boarding, or canvas, stretched on iron roller side-boards on the sheds.

The finest of the vessels seen to be visiting Liverpool were the American packet ships – particularly the British and North American steamships such as the Arcadia, the Britannia and the Columbia – reputedly able to carry the mail from Liverpool to Halifax, or Boston, in about fourteen days. They contrasted with other, slower, 'short-run' steamers such as those of the Glasgow line, the Dublin line, the Isle of Man line and the Cork line.

This regular and rapid source of communication, particularly with North America, helped Liverpool to become Europe's principal departure point. Emigrants, seeking opportunities in Canada and the United States, flocked to the port as did thousands of others seeking to travel to Australia and New Zealand. Thus, whilst the quaysides might be littered with tar barrels, tea chests, and tobacco casks, the streets were constantly filled with long caravans laden with merchandise and travellers. The cart drivers and their passengers passed numerous establishments where makers of seafaring equipment, such as rope-walks, chain cables and sail canvas plied their trades. Near these they might also pass steam boat and steam engine works, oil mills, sugar refineries and bakehouses for ships' biscuits and other essentials.

Among the visitors to the heart of the seafront, the pierheads, were those who might then seek out the different flags hoisted there so that they might more easily find the Glasgow boat, the Isle of Man boat, those for Dublin, Cork, Pembroke and the outstandingly popular flag of Bangor for those wishing to visit North Wales. None could have remained unimpressed by the feverish activity there and the innumerable smoking funnels of various steamers hastening to and from Liverpool.

Never far from such Victorian visitors, however, were the unsolicited dangers presented by the many local beggars and thieves. Not far from the docks themselves any strangers might stray, or be lured, into one of the many densely populated localities in the great lines of streets that ran parallel to the docks.

Here they might meet with whole districts composed of streets filled with boarding houses, lodging houses, beershops, gin palaces, singing saloons, huxters' shops and the like. Whilst in these streets they might walk down narrow passageways, or alleys, and enter the cramped courtyards packed with smaller houses. Beneath many of these houses, both large and small, they might see the tops of doorways which led into the infamous cellar dwellings of the seaport.

Within the crowded confines of the narrow courts, the entrances of which 'morning noon and night' were thronged with people, they might find hosts of slatternly women. Sailors' lodginghouses abounded within these courts and they were usually marked by their 'cooking for shipping' signs. Many portions of these districts of the port in time, moreover, were to become thickly studded by undisguised displays of vice in its grossest features.

2

The Prince Consort opens the Albert Dock

When Prince Albert sailed into the new Liverpool Dock that was to be named in his honour, he entered into the very heart of the seaport known to many as the 'Gateway to the West'. He and those of his affluent companions who engaged in the expensive celebrations, on Thursday 30th July 1846, had the opportunity to hear about some of the proposed wealth of merchandise that was to be protectively stored in the imposing five stacks of warehouses surrounding the quayside of the enclosed dock.

The Prince proceeded into the Dock, from the River Mersey, on board the Royal Yacht Fairy. Both on the River and in the Dock he was greeted rapturously. Liverpudlians had crowded onto vessels of almost every description to catch sight of him whilst he was on the river. Inside the dock some 10,000 invited guests thronged the quaysides. Later on the same day Prince Albert joined a special gathering of 1,000 guests in a symbolically decorated warehouse room. Mr. Troutbeck of Hanover Square, London, had specially prepared this as a venue for a grand luncheon.

"The pillars and arched brick ceilings were painted of

stone colour, the pillars being ornamented with gold bands which encircled the capitals. The walls were glazed with calico, fluted in alternate colours of pink, blue and white. The hangings to the windows were the same with white drapery and pink rosettes, the division below the arches at the windows being fitted with purple moulding".

Many seeing the newly built warehouses would have been able to appreciate, at first hand, the ability of the dock trust staff to cater efficiently for the arrival of scores of deep-sea trading ships, from the Far East, India and the Americas. These Albert Dock staff had no legal requirement to wait for excise men, but could themselves speedily discharge the ships' cargoes for sorting and sampling inside the voluminous warehouse stacks. Furthermore, they had no reason to risk leaving the vulnerable cargoes, such as tea, silk, hemp, cotton, sugar, spirits and tobacco, exposed on the dock's quaysides.

The merchant guests at the opening ceremony saw further advantages, too, for they only had to pay duties on their stored goods when they sold them. They also could instruct their ships' captains to manoeuvre their empty vessels to the adjacent Salthouse Dock. Here they took on outward bound bulk cargoes such as coal, salt and railway iron for shipment to India, Brazil, Mexico, the West Indies, or even to the east coast of the U.S.A.

In their elegant clothes, both the royal party and the other specially invited guests contrasted starkly with many raggedly dressed people who lived in and worked just beyond the new complex. Hundreds of these less fortunate people may have felt that the infamous districts near the dock were better collectively described as the 'Black Spot on the Mersey'.

Those wealthy Liverpool citizens who enthusiastically applauded the Prince as he sailed around the dock had come to see a development that was not only a magnificent example of public commercial enterprise, but one they believed would be a major turning point in their fight against local fireraisers. They also expected by using it they would be able to frustrate the hordes of thieves who had long preyed on the more open Liverpool docklands.

Over many years preceding the inauguration, the city councillors and their wealthy business supporters had been particularly disturbed by the large number of destructive and explosive warehouse fires. Some of these had been started accidentally by careless seafarers and dock labourers but others had been deliberately caused by Liverpool incendiaries. In 1838 and in 1842, as we shall see in more detail later, Liverpool's dockland dwellers came to experience some of the port's most horrendous fires. In the latter year, those merchants who had invested in the likes of the Crompton Street property and that in Great Howard Street, Formby Street and Neptune Street saw much of it totally ruined. They vigorously lobbied the city councillors to make the warehouse architects improve their designs, the builders their techniques and the firepolicemen their vigilance.

The Royal yacht entering the Albert Dock.

The Dejeuner, at the Albert Dock.

His Royal Highness Prince Albert leaving the dock.

In 1843, the year the contract to begin the Albert Dock warehouse was awarded, the city magistrates had, on June 24th, demanded that the mayor should meet the members of the watch committee. He was pleased to hear the members agree that they would provide fifty extra constables for the policeforce and that they in turn would become responsible for ensuring greater security against the warehouse arsonists. The same watch committee members voiced their satisfaction that a system for the registration of warehouses, based on their fireproofing merits, was also to be introduced.

They must also have been reassured by the special fireproofing features that were planned for the Albert Dock warehouses. These safeguards of course had been thoroughly tested by Jesse Hartley the Liverpool Dock engineer in his trials on models. Between 1841 and 1843 he had prepared six different designs of warehouses to be made of fireproof or semi-fireproof construction.

Hartley eventually convinced the Dock Board Trustees of the obvious merits of a non-traditional design composed of brick and iron for the new Albert Dock warehouses. In 1843 he had models of arches of different types erected in the Coburg Dockyard and he unsuccessfully tried to have them broken down by fire. At the Trentham Street Dockyard he then had barrels of tar, pitch and split wood ignited to test both a model with brick arches between iron columns and beams and a timber building model which was lined with sheet iron.

His brick and iron structure proved overwhelmingly successful under these experimental conditions. Herein lay the basis of the success of the Albert Dock which was finally built to contain an area of seven and three-quarter acres of water and was to house the five massive warehouse stacks constructed entirely of incombustible materials, i.e. cast iron, brick and granite.

From the point of view of royal security, the watch committee too must have been particularly impressed by their merit since they knew from bitter experience that the Liverpool firefighters would not have been quickly able to overcome any major fire if one had started when the Prince was at the riverfront.

They must have been grateful too, that the many thousands of immigrants in Liverpool at that time, particularly the Irish, would have been unable to encroach near the dock and embarrass the Prince by their political protestations. Some had been forced to stay in the seaport when they could not afford to pay their shipping brokers for passage to continue on their way overseas. In time they often became unmanageable in their diseased and crime-ridden quarters. In a three day period, in June 1841, the Irish carpenters and casual dock labourers supported by their thousands of destitute acquaintances, had caused havoc in their Anti-Corn Law protests on a hitherto unknown scale.

When Prince Albert had completed his visit the city guardians demanded the dock should have its own special protective force of constables. To fully safeguard the dock and all its newly built quays and warehouses, in 1846, they had the watch committee send a special body of twenty-one constables to patrol it.

These constables had to guard the dock exclusively, even though their head constable, Maurice Dowling, complained that another seventy police walks, in less fashionable parts of the port, had been left without a constable to patrol them.

These constables became an impressive presence on their tours of duty in the dock. They wore the expensive but somewhat uncomfortable Liverpool police uniform. Each of their black, glazed top hats had an inner protective support but was cumbersome. At the same time, too, the navy blue military tunic, with its heavily kilted 'skirt', quickly absorbed rain.

To complete his uniform, each constable wore a pair of grey woollen pants and a heavy pair of boots. Each also carried a heavy walking stick and a rattle for signalling. In an emergency, he was expected to unbuckle his outer leather waistbelt and strap the legs, or arms, of any violent prisoner.

Thus these policemen gave vital additional security to a complex consisting of five warehouse stacks almost entirely surrounded by a high perimeter wall. Where there was no outer wall, in the north east angle of the site, the police helped to supervise the opening and closing of the huge, iron, cartbay doors.

They surveyed the perimeter wall openings from their purpose-built watch huts. They knew that any person moving inside this wall, but outside the warehouses would be confined to the outer yard of each individual stack. Once inside the stacks the users had their freedom of movement restricted by the limited number of staircases. There was only one staircase in each of the north, the north-east and the south-east stacks, two in the south-east and four in the west stack which was entirely fronted by the River Mersey.

By such measures the warehouse users must have felt, therefore, that they had made a major stand against the fireraisers and criminals who ravaged the Liverpool docks. The law breakers, both adult and children alike, had found much to encourage their decision to live upon the proceeds of their daily life of crime. They accepted stealing as a vital part of their life there. Many of them had grown up in a tradition of stealing from the abundant quantities of goods that the merchants often had to leave unattended on the quaysides.

The thieves grew in numbers as the port grew and as the Liverpool merchants became the second most important major exporters in Great Britain. Between 1801 and 1831 those persons who lived in Liverpool had more than doubled their numbers. Hence, 165,000 persons were known to live, by the latter year, within the borough boundaries. Another 80,000 came to join these within the next ten years.

Just beyond the Albert Dock, hosts of vagabond children, immigrants, visiting sailors, dock labourers, drunkards, prostitutes and thieves came to realise that their future lay in their ability to find their way successfully through the docklands that stretched along the River Mersey. Many unable to do so, quickly found that their life in Liverpool became a living hell.

Many others, who were more fortunate, came to visit the seafront for a short, quite innocent, time only. They did so increasingly when the railway owners began to offer cheap travel in the mid-forties. On 13th July, 1845 more than 5,000 arrived, early on the Sunday morning, from Manchester. A week later another 7,000 came, overcrowding all the main thoroughfares from the Edge Hill Railway Station to the docks, from early morning until midnight. Many of them also embarked on the vessels that sailed to the Mersey Light Ship and back again. Others no doubt, made use of such cheap train services, in 1846, to travel in the hope of seeing Prince Albert pass into Liverpool.

In time, such day-trippers, and those living and working on the seafront, became relieved to notice the improvements there. Over forty years later, Queen Victoria, herself, came nostalgically to visit the riverfront and she saw a Liverpool dockland that had changed for the better. Her Majesty journeyed by open carriage to the pierheads on the second day of her three-day state visit to Liverpool, 11-13 May, 1886. She was intent on enjoying her visit to that part of the river dominated by the Albert Dock.

She carried out her entire programme riding in an open carriage, even through drenching rain, protected only by a relay of open umbrellas held over her. She proceeded to St. George's Hall by a circuitous route and then went on to the Landing Stage, where she embarked on the steamer Claughton. So popular was she in Liverpool on this occasion that, at their own special request, the dock and town policemen removed their helmets and joined in the cheers of the crowds as Her Majesty passed them.

The arrival of the Royal Yacht, 30 July 1846
Prince Albert and his retinue arrive at the dock gate entrance to the Canning Half-Tide Dock. Whilst some 10,000 guests awaited his entry to the Albert Dock, the River Mersey was crowded with vessels. Aboard these, as shown, cheering admirers attempt to catch a glimpse of him aboard the Royal Yacht Fairy. St Nicholas' Church and the Custom House are clearly visible amongst the array of flags and bunting in this fine print.

3

Warehouse and Dockland Firefighters

When the city councillors celebrated with Prince Albert at his opening of the new Liverpool dock, they were well aware the dock firefighters had never been truly effective in their attempts to overcome major dockland fires. The principal firefighters were only a very small band of dock constables who, after 1836, had also accepted a paltry payment for their part-time firefighting duties.

These men had to be ready, whenever necessary in the thirties to help operate any of the seaport's manual fire-engines, such as the three kept at the north end of Prince's Dock. At first, they undertook little if any firefighting practice, although they had to deal with most of the expensive fires as they blazed in the docklands. To help remedy this, after the town and dock constables became amalgamated in 1836, twenty extra constables found themselves being added for fire duties to the dock division strength. These knew when they accepted the additional responsibility of fire "bobby", the nickname Sir Robert Peel's men had originally received, they would be paid only an extra shilling each week to act in this capacity.

They and their colleagues usually could do little when

The Great Fire, 15 January 1833
Crowds begin to gather to witness many warehouses ablaze in the Bath Street and
New Quay sections of the Dock Road. The Prince's Dock and George's Dock with
the nearby St. Nicholas' Church are clearly visible. This view of the Great Fire, on the
morning of 15 January 1883, indicates how property to the amount of £250,000 was
destroyed

Liverpool Fire Brigade hand-drawn equipment, 1890
Liverpool's Victorian Firemen often had to haul heavy equipment like that shown in
the photograph to the fire face without the assistance of horses. The hand-drawn
hose and ladder was part of the reserve equipment kept at the police fire stations in
the docks and the city.

they ran all the way, in full uniform, to a serious ship or explosive warehouse fire. They quickly realised they only had crude equipment to operate against the fiercest of blazes. They tackled a monumental one in Robert Street North, in October, 1838 which they believed was one of the worst they had ever seen in the docklands. It was comparable to that which had occurred in the Bath Street, New Quay and Lancelot's Hey district, in 1833, when property valued at £250,000 was destroyed. Initially, they found the 1838 fire spread quickly when they could not locate an adequate water supply to put it out.

They arrived at the fire, attached their standcocks to the nearest fire plugs but no water flowed out. Then they quickly used up their own water cart supply. Their admirable leader, Superintendent Hewitt, did manage to supply one engine from the nearby canal and he also drew seawater from the docks but he found the pressure was too weak. At the height of the fire, when one of his brave men climbed with his firehose onto a warehouse roof, Head Constable Michael Whitty and the Superintendent joined him. The branchman, however, did not realise he had not unscrewed his firehose nozzle. When he called down to the engine operator to play up the water, his leather hose burst.

Even when the Mayor came to help in the operations he could do little at this fire. By the time the firefighters got twelve manual engines into full play, they could only bring five hoses to bear on the inferno because of the distance their water had to travel from its source. Those at

the scene saw it as one of indescribable alarm and
confusion. The hordes of onlookers gasped as all the
warehouses in Robert Street together with the fine ones
between the cotton shed and Waterloo Road became
doomed to total destruction. Whitty himself felt helpless
in trying to deal with the dangerous explosives there:

*"the question being where it would stop: an explosion of salt
petre in one warehouse was followed by a second explosion from
the ruins it was an awful one: we stood as it were under a dome
of fire, flame, cotton bags and ignited missiles. The doors and
windows of the houses in the adjoining street were either
smashed or carried away; and all around appeared in flames."*

Whitty had more than twice as many firefighters to use in
this disaster than at any previous Liverpool warehouse
fire but he knew they were totally inadequate. His men
began their efforts at nine o'clock on a Friday evening and
could not extinguish the flames until Sunday morning.
They valued the destroyed property at £120,000.

His men consistently faced the handicap of being unable
to find a strong water supply especially when they first
arrived at the scene of a fire.

Liverpool's firefighters had to wait another nine years, in
fact, before the water supply was taken out of private
hands. Nor did the firemen alone suffer for, as in other
British seaports, the poor of Liverpool begged for water,
stole it and engaged in daily brawls over it.

At another even more horrendous dockland fire, in 1842, when the men raced to Crompton Street, they found the hurricane force wind scattering their hose water in an ineffective spray. In desperation they opened a sewer in their attempt to find an ample supply. The firemen saw such a rapid spread of fire that warehouse after warehouse collapsed. So much so that a few minutes after they arrived they saw that all of the adjacent Formby Street had become a crater of fire. After the fire they reporterd several sheds, a cooperage and a wheelright's yard in Crompton Street as being consumed. Walking along the adjoining dockside routes, through Great Howard Street they also saw two cotton sheds had fallen. In Formby Street eleven warehouses, and in Neptune Street two more cotton sheds, a cooperage and two rice sheds had fallen in ruins. In all 48,000 bales of cotton insured at £384,000 were destroyed. Nevertheless, they found on their journey that one fire-proof warehouse had remained standing at the very centre of the holocaust. A lesson, no doubt, that helped dock engineers in the future, including Jesse Hartley in his planning of the Albert Dock warehouses.

Liverpool folk, both affluent and penniless, expressed their sense of anger about the senselessness of the inferno they had witnessed in the Crompton Street district. A great upsurge of hostile public opinion forced the warehouse owners, fire insurance agents, the magistrates and the watch committee members to alter radically their ideas on warehouse protection and construction.

Liverpool Fire Brigade Steamer, 1898
Crowds line William Brown Street to witness the steam fire engine 'Hornby' outside
the Liverpool Museum and central library. The powerful-looking team of four horses
draws the engine with the impressively uniformed officers aboard, across the tram
lines that curve past a corner of St. John's Gardens. This extraordinary steamer
reputedly had a capability of 1600 gallons per minute at this time.

John Hewitt, Liverpool's first Brigade Superintendent
John Hewitt, the first Superintendent of Liverpool's Fire Brigade stands wearing his
distinctive top hat and medals, at the side of the Merryweather steam fire-engine,
the Clint, 1865. The attendant policemen wear the early 19th-century uniform as
they proudly parade with Liverpool's first 'steamer' which had a capability of
delivering 510 gallons of water per minute

Forced by the complaints from the public at large, the Liverpool magistrates openly expressed the view that they had become deeply disturbed by the recent widespread incendiaries' activities in the Liverpool docklands. They brought matters to a head in June 1843 when they demanded that the mayor should attend a meeting of the watch committee on the 24th of that month.

In heated exchanges they urged that the watch committee should instantly add to the police force fifty extra constables so that that number of men could be immediately sent into the borough warehouses to provide them with greater protection. They called upon the watch committee members, in no uncertain terms, to implement rigorously the provisions of the Liverpool Warehouse Bill passed in the same year.

The watch committee, in turn, then formally approached the Head Constable, Michael Whitty, and asked him to send out the fifty men at once into the warehouses. Whitty's response, after carefully considering the already heavy demands on his men, was to direct two inspectors and forty constables to patrol the warehouses during the coldest and darkest days of the year, from September to March. When dock people lit fewer fires, from April to August, he reduced their numbers to thirty-two constables to patrol their special beats. Each member of this warehouse watch expected to patrol for about nine hours each day. They particularly looked to prevent any warehousemen from operating dangerous fire-using processes in unsuitable warehouses and had to further ensure that dock labourers did not move high risk combustible stores into any other vulnerable buildings.

So successfully did these constables operate in the first year of their patrols that they helped significantly to reduce the number of explosive and destructive fires. Undoubtedly, those who formally invited the Prince Consort to Liverpool must have been greatly re-assured by this news.

They must also have been heartened that the Liverpool authorities had demanded that the warehouse owners should play a much more responsible role in protecting their own property. They, thus, directed the owners to use all their available resources to prevent any future outbreak of fire and they were to ensure particularly that such outbreaks that did happen did not spread from one warehouse to the next. Therein they felt the architects could, in part, achieve this by improving future warehouse design.

Advancing their ideas, the authorities wholeheartedly supported the introduction of an effective system for registering all Liverpool's dockland warehouses. In this they approved the use of three clearly defined categories of warehouse; those entirely built of fireproof construction which used brick and cast iron and contained no timber, those which had external fireproofing, being constructed of brick with window frames of iron, and those which received the classification of being built before 1843.

Those fire insurance companies' officers working at the docks also quickly recognised the value of such registrations and offered considerably reduced premiums to the owners of registered warehouses with fireproof construction provided throughout. Undoubtedly, Prince Albert opened a dock complex that offered the most up to date fireproofing facilities in Liverpool at that time.

When the Prince arrived, therefore, the magistrates, the watch committee members and the head constable must have been thankful for these improvements and the vigilance of the warehouse patrols. They had little doubt that if his safety had been left to depend entirely on the Liverpool fire-bobbies the Prince would have placed himself at some risk.

Only three full-time firemen, sixty-one part-time firemen and those casual labourers randomly recruited at the scene of a fire could have answered a summons to help at a major fire. The three permanent firemen moreover, had to repair and clean all Liverpool's scattered firefighting equipment. They had to travel considerable distances, usually on foot, in both the town and the docklands and often had to move by their own physical exertions the extremely cumbersome equipment that was weighed down by gunmetal fittings.

Their principal officer, Superintendent Hewitt, lived, at this time, at the central station, Temple Court. This was quite far from the docks. To summon all the firefighters he ordered his men to ring the alarm bell there for half an hour when they heard of a serious fire outbreak. Some men, no doubt, needed this time just to travel to the central station. In this event, the engine drivers, who slept above an adjoining stable, would have to harness the horses they required from the ten kept there. Hewitt then sent out a maximum of seven engines and six small water carts. In addition, some of the men would have to pull the hand-drawn carriages on which each kept their stand pipes, plug irons, and 150 yards of fire hose. They also had to bring one twenty-ton water tank to refill the water carts, as necessary.

At the docks themselves, the bridewell keepers took charge of a total of eight engines and six water carts, stationing five engines at the north dock stations and three at the south dock stations. When they met with extreme water supply failure, the bridewell keepers at the Vauxhall Station and the north dock station each had one six-ton water tank to dispatch as a last resort.

Two years before Prince Albert arrived, Head Constable Henry Miller, had eight new lighter water carts, each capable of conveying 160 gallons of water, purchased for use by his fire constables. He ordered his men to keep their water carts filled and further instructed them that they keep their horses constantly harnessed so that they could haul the new carts to a fire before the engines arrived.

He also sent men with special pipe carriages that they had laden with spare hose, pipescaling ladders, common

Liverpool Fire Brigade, 'Holt' steamer, 1899
Chief Superintendent J. J. Thomas who was highly praised for his fire engine experiments at the Albert Dock, in 1897, is seen supervising the Merryweather steamer 'Holt'. This machine, claimed by the makers to be the most powerful land steam fire engine in the world was capable of delivering 1800 gallons per minute.

Liverpool's 'Hornby' steamer, 1898
This steam fire engine, 'Hornby', was used by Chief Inspector Thomas to take water directly from the Albert Dock mains water pipes. The crew of the fire engine are shown making use of the Hornby's self-contained refreshment box as they direct the efficicient use of the fire engine amid billows of steam.

ladders, crow bars, hammers, torches, keys, ropes and the like. To overcome the casual labourers' fraudulent claims at the scene of the fire, he insisted on the use of a copper engraving plate he had had purchased for printing labourers' time tickets.

One year later, in 1845, Maurice Dowling accepted the post of Chief Constable and had to make the arrangements for Prince Albert's safety at the dock. He began a series of steady improvements in his men's firefighting activities.

They began to use newer and more dependable equipment and had to carry out regular fire drill exercises for fixing apparatus and for supplying water. Sometimes they even used Liverpool's new supply of high pressure water at the scenes of fire whenever they knew that the necessary underground pipes had been laid. They also adopted the advanced London style suits of fireproof clothing and fire-escape equipment.

Thus, by the time Dowling saw the Prince arrive at the Albert Dock the Liverpool firemen had steadily improved their efficiency compared to that of their predecessors those of some fifteen years earlier. In spite of these improvements they could still be overtaken by large-scale disasters such as those that befell them in 1856 when they could not contain a series of raging fires at the North Shore Cotton Factory. They did not acquire a steam-powered fire engine until 1865.

When they brought into commission the latter they eagerly put it to regular use at the docks. They owed this breakthrough to Head Constable John Greig, who travelled to London's metropolitan station at Watling Street, to inspect and recommend the purchase of a £600 land engine. When he saw the London demonstration he realised his men could comfortably fit a steam engine on board a boat if they needed to tackle a fire on the river.

In a matter of weeks they became expert at operating and moving this three-ton engine, which they affectionately called the Clint, complete with its coal and water. At the fire face they delighted that in ten minutes they could raise ten pounds of steam pressure from it. To do this they had to kindle a good size wood and coal fire to heat the cold water boiler. Four minutes later they aimed to increase the steam pressure as high as seventy pounds and using two ⅞ inch jets, or nozzles, each supplied from a separate hose, they succeeded in raising water jets some 130 feet in height.

Not surprisingly these firefighters steadily won local and national admirers. Charles Dickens wrote in support of them in his The Uncommercial Traveller: "I had entered the Liverpool Police Force . . . its organisation, against fires, I can take to be much better than the Metropolitan System".

The Liverpool fire bobbies, in turn, then began to train their own fire engine stokers, they used gas jets on the engine boilers to further quicken their steam pressure rise and began to offer contracts to secure a supply of better horses to haul their engines.

In time they appreciated, too, that when the Clint suffered a breakdown, as it did in March 1873, they needed a reserve engine. Returning from a town fire at St. Michael's Church, West Derby Road, the Clint's crew experienced one of the large rear wheels giving way at the foot of the steep hill in London Road. Certain that his men, using this type of engine, could cope with any serious fire, Greig asked that at least one more be purchased for his men to operate at the north docks where they felt the growing need to protect the petroleum sheds, timber yards and the heavy tonnage of shipping at risk from fire.

By this time the men had won for themselves the reputation of being the finest in the Liverpool Police Force and distinguished themselves by their strength, fine physique, agility and coolness when facing danger. They achieved this distinction in the eighties when the firemen still had to run all the way to the nearest police station in the event of a fire. They also had to shout the message to any constable they passed in their dash. For a very serious fire a constable could summon a taxi cab and shout the alarm as he rode on top in its outer box.

By this date, however, only a total of eleven firefighters could still at first be sent to a major fire from the central fire station. Even at this stage when the exhausted men returned they could not bathe, find a suitable changing room, dry out their clothing or enjoy any recreational facilities for none were provided for them.

Firemen Turncocks, c 1879
These firemen are wearing the expensive, but somewhat uncomfortable, Liverpool police uniform, c 1879. The navy blue tunic, with its heavily kilted skirt, quickly absorbed water and was regarded as 'old-fashioned' by the 1880's. The firemen's long beards and thick waist belts also became unfashionable and disappeared towards the end of the century.

4

Constables, Cutlasses and Cholera

For many years, at the beginning of the nineteenth century, those travelling into Liverpool by way of the River Mersey could expect scant protection from Liverpool's constables. Indeed, several badly organised bodies of constables operated independently on the waterfront. Dock watchmen, dock gatemen and corporation constables openly clashed as arch rivals.

The smallest group, the corporation constables could sometimes be seen at the centre of Liverpool's riverfront. They operated outside the docks at the pierheads. Their superintendent, who lived in their headquarters in Exchange Street East, sent out a body of them each day to the riverside.

Here they had to collect those fees paid by the deep water and cross river ferry passengers for the use of a crane to haul their luggage and baggage ashore from berthing vessels. These constables should have been strictly supervised but were not, for some of them frequently visited a nearby grog shop whilst on duty. Others, using their comfortable, stone lodging house at the pierheads, constantly sat around the fire there. They only stirred themselves to earn tips by rushing to carry gentlemen's parcels, topcoats and luggage as they came ashore after crossing the Mersey.

At some distance either side of the pierheads, the dock watchmen and independent dock gatemen were called upon to protect the north and south docks, but they did not. The dock watchmen accepted their appointment from the dock watch committee, a council body whose members probably first met in 1815 when the Dock Police Office was built.

Although the members of the full Liverpool Council retained overall control of the dock estate, having been responsible for developing the construction of Liverpool docks from 1708, the separate sub-committee members, or dock watch, directed dock affairs. From 1826 their thirteen councillors, together with eight dockside rate-payers under a chairman formed this sub-committee.

Over the years the dock watch members did little to improve their constables' dreadful behaviour and independent outlook. They heard constant complaints that these constables and those of the town bickered and showed their intense jealousy of each other by refusing to exchange information or communicate in any helpful manner. At the same time they took little disciplinary action. Indeed, drunken dock watchmen had become notorious for breaking out into fits of fighting with their rivals in the town watch. Some dock watchmen had even locked up the town policemen in the dock bridewells, causing the town police walks to become unprotected.

The Canning Dock and Custom House, c 1910
This picture shows th Canning dock filled with sailing ships and Mersey flat boats. The Custom House, which dominates the centre skyline, was situated in front of the Sailors' Home in Canning Place. This district was notorious for its 'land traps' for sailors in the Victorian hey day of the sailing ship. The transit shed visible behind the vessels had the simple function of protecting inward or outward-bound cargoes from the weather

Old George's Dock, c 1903
This busy corner of George's Dock reflects the activity associated with it when it was the centre of the important fruit trade in Liverpool. In this picture the eastern quayside skyline is dominated by the Tower Building and St. Nicholas' Church. Among the many sailing craft features shown is the custom of raising canvas to 'dry out' sails.

Their poor behaviour could no longer be tolerated by the thirties, however, as the need for protection at the many new docks grew. After an alarming series of outrageous complaints the dock committee members reacted drastically. In November, 1832, they followed the town watch example and appointed a former London policeman, Maurice Dowling, to improve the dock watchmen.

As superintendent of the dock police from 1833 to 1836, he directed his men on the basis of his experience in the capital. He particularly tried to prepare them to cope with the increasing everyday emergencies they had to face at the docks. Hence, when any person fell into the crowded docks, for example, he had his men help the unfortunates and had them use the hot water, beds and other necessities that he asked the dock watch to provide in the public houses adjacent to the docks.

In his three years as superintendent, though his men still came to witness death by drowning of thirty-one desperate persons in the different docks and seven persons in the River Mersey, he delighted that they also saw three hundred and seven persons rescued. He and his men helped save these lives, moreover, even though they could look for help from just two small Liverpool lifeboats since the Cheshire inhabitants had none on their entire coast.

However, any of his attempts to have his watchmen cooperate with the town police were openly rejected by the dock watch because they jealously guarded any attempts to infringe on the private owners' rights at the docks. They argued that since the pay and accessories (like watchboxes and lockup houses) of Dowling's men had not been provided by public means they should remain under strict private control.

Nevertheless, the two bodies of constables found themselves being organised more and more as one police force, after 1835, when the Municipal Corporation's Bill was passed. The first Head Constable of Liverpool Michael Whitty, formerly the superintendent of the town watch, worked energetically to unify the several rival constabularies and he helped achieve a temporary union in 1836 when he acted decisively in the matter. He renamed all Liverpool policemen as general borough constables. Then he had the symbolic anchor insignia, previously worn by the dock policemen on their tunic collar, removed and replaced with that of the city liver bird. He then numbered all the constables consecutively and drew up the conditions of service for a combined force.

Whitty effectively reorganised the dock police using as a model Sir Robert Peel's London police reforms. Most importantly, having promoted Maurice Dowling to take charge of recruitment, he left control of the dock constables in the hands of one officer, Superintendent George Tyrrel. Whitty helped him to establish his command at the central dock station, in James Street, several hundred yards from the district later to house the

Albert Dock. Furthermore, he gave him general control over both the firefighters in the town and those in the docks.

Tyrrel's ordinary dock policemen however, found their new duties to be extremely severe being expected to fully carry out an average of twelve hours' work each day. Each was also entitled to only three days leave of absence with pay. They had no weekday holiday either.

Nor did they as yet receive any worthwhile help from the independent body of dock gatemen. To leave, or enter the dock estate from the town side, immigrants, casual labourers, drivers of horse-drawn vehicles, sailors and the like, usually had to pass through the imposing twin towered gateways set in the prison-like, stone boundary walls.

Until November 1838, however, a weakwilled and ineffective group of dock gatemen open to bribery, bullying and laziness, became by day and by night the only overseers of all the hundreds of persons who might pass in or out through the dock gateways. Like the constables, they often had in their ranks men who had been dismissed from other constabularies for misconduct.

This band of eighty-eight men became duly sworn in as borough constables in 1838 and, as before, had to receive their meagre pay from the dock committee. When they had their traditional 'topper' style hats re-labelled 'dockgateman and constable', they at last took a first step to becoming responsible guardians for the vast tonnage of goods that daily passed outside their tower watchposts. They now had the power to stop, search and question any adult and child they suspected of stealing from the docks.

Their fine superiors, the members of the dock trust and those of the watch committee nevertheless still wrangled with cynical jealousy until 1841. Then the assize judges appointed a barrister to arbitrate between them. The judges at last enabled the Liverpool town clerk to report in June of that year, that the constables of the united town and dock service had to be sworn in by the watch committee without reference to the dock committee.

The watch committee reforms of the thirties, faced increasing strains in the forties. In this, the decade of the cutlass and bludgeon, their constables had to come to terms with an evergrowing swell of local political and social upheaval. Catholic Irish immigrants led the vanguard. Irish carpenters and labourers readily clashed at the docks with their Orange Order counterparts. The Irish felt the Corn Laws had forced them to leave their own land and had deprived them of cheap food. In Liverpool, once destitute, they felt unable to apply for relief, at the parish workhouse. Their daily contempt grew and in extreme cases they armed themselves with bludgeons. In June 1841, they clashed with the police in their thousands over a period of three days.

Matters boiled over and Head Constable Whitty had to call out policemen mounted on the fire brigade horses, when bands of Irish carpenters began to assemble at the docks. At Seel Street station he armed an entire division of his men with cutlasses and sent them to Canning Dock. They arrived just in time to meet a body of 3,000 labourers marching from the Graving Docks. Whitty remonstrated with his fellow countrymen and when they refused to obey him and halt, he deployed his men, cutlasses at the ready, across James Street and forced the labourers to retreat. After seeing the Mayor they finally dispersed.

Nevertheless, the entire police force, helped by the dock gatemen, the Chelsea pensioners and the town's scavengers, was kept at the ready. In other serious incidents the policemen came under pistol shot, faced more bludgeon attacks and even the head constable only narrowly escaped from serious injury when he fell from his horse as it slipped in a chasing of the rioters.

In the year before Prince Albert came to the famous Liverpool dock, the Irish immigrants came in record numbers to swamp the port in a human tidal wave. They stretched the resources of many, including the police, to breaking point. Attempting to escape the consequences of their own potato famine which commenced in 1845, they desperately believed that Liverpool was the gateway to a better life. Many of them arrived as paupers, stayed and settled in the poorest quarters of the seaport, near the docks.

Some of these unfortunates congregated in the dirty lodging houses and became apathetic about their cleanliness and toilet habits. Others dossed in the filthiest and worst-ventilated courtyard houses and cellars.

The first accommodation to be used was usually that of the lodging house or cellars in the 'front' dockland streets. These streets also contained many passageways that led into the 'back' courtyards which had even smaller houses built around them.

Many of the larger front lodging houses and the smaller ones in the courtyards had cellars beneath them that were opened as separate units of accommodation. So bad had the quality of life become in these districts, by 1840, that the average span of life for those living there, was but 15 years.

In 1842, John Finch Junior, on behalf of the Anti-Monopoly Association, a free trade organisation, carried out a very exhaustive investigation into the economic circumstances of the families living in the Vauxhall ward. 1842 was a depression year. Out of 4,814 families he found 1,342 to be without visible income, whilst the average weekly earnings was only nine shillings and threepence per family. A further 1,052 families, he recognised, supported themselves by pawning, prostitution or charity.

The pressure from the immigrants in such districts, was relentless. Some 300,000 Irish are believed to have landed in the first six months of 1847. Some 60,000 to 80,000 sought refuge in the cheapest lodging houses, in the

Sergeant Pavey at Prince's Dock, 1901
By the middle of the 19th century the Prince's Dock was reputedly the most magnificent of Liverpool's docks. It was particularly famous for receiving the finest sailing ships from India and China as well as the largest of the North American vessels. Behind Dock Police Sergeant Pavey in this photograph the use of the dock by both steam and sail-powered coastal vessels is evident.

courthouses, or in the cellar dwellings like those to be found in Ashton Street, Bedford Street and Duckinfield Street (near Liverpool's Brownlow Hill workhouse). Although 3,000 of the worst cellars had been closed with police help, after the 1842 Liverpool Improvement Act, they were re-opened again as the waves of immigrants became desperate for refuge. In total more than one million of these people landed in Liverpool between 1849 and 1853. Germans and Italians joined them in large numbers and swelled the immigrant dockside queues for passage to North America or to the Colonies.

Those looking for lodging houses as temporary accommodation close to the docks found them in the web of streets interwoven throughout the sailors' quarters in the likes of Wapping, Canning Street, Paradise Street, Cleveland Square, Park Lane and Lower Parliament Street. Often those already sheltered thieves, vagabonds and loose women.

Gin palaces, beer vaults, huxters' shops and similar establishments stood adjacent to these filthy-looking and ramshackle tenements. Outside on the steps of those houses with the familiar 'lodgings' sign, sat crowds of ill-clad, shoeless and dirt-encrusted men, women and children. Usually only those visitors bold enough in manner could force entry past such groups. Irishmen again reputedly provided the worst lodgings for the vagabonds, the vagrants and their fellow countrymen in these districts.

Many of these who could not afford to continue on their passage of emigration had no choice but to trudge up to those tenements situated in the back courts which were only five yards wide.

Frequently, the tenements were seen to be four storeys high, 'straight up and down', containing four apartments, namely a cellar, a living room and two bedrooms. In such buildings, two or three families had to seek shelter. At the top of the court, without a single toilet, they had to use the open cesspool or privy.

By 1847, moreover, in different districts of the city, 50 to 60 destitute people regularly had to share a house with only three or four small rooms each about twelve feet by ten in size. In more than one instance upwards of 40 persons were found living in a basement cellar.

In these desperate years of immigration the police focused their attention on the humble riverfront wards and particularly on their infamous lodging houses and cellars. After the 1842 Liverpool Improvement Bill was passed, they did manage to register and check many of the houses of an inferior description. By 1847 they had helped to establish that Liverpool had about 450 of these 'common' lodging houses. Some seventy-five police inspectors and sergeants assisted the health committee in its attempt to make these better places of residence.

The police became so thoroughly unpopular in their lodging house inspections, especially at night when they found them to be most overcrowded, that they welcomed the termination of this duty. The officers themselves resented this unpaid extra duty, too, for it often led them to neglect the supervision of their own constables. Therefore they heartily welcomed the recommendation, in 1859, that the specially appointed body of sanitary officers, controlled by the health committee, be solely responsible for this unpleasant task.

Liverpool's constables similarly disliked having to report the re-opening of the condemned cellars, but Dr. W. H. Duncan, Liverpool's first medical officer of health, regarded their work in this respect as invaluable. This was not the first time the men had helped to provide information about the port's cellar dwellings because in August, 1844, they had helped to record that in those twelve wards forming the parish of Liverpool some 20,168 inhabitants lived in 6,924 'front' street cellars (this figure was exclusive of those persons using the court cellars).

Usually only the poorest of all emigrants took their families into the court cellars. Often they discovered that they were badly ventilated, windowless shelters less than six feet in height, with about ten or twelve square feet of flagstones or bare earth. Some of the families in the most overcrowded areas, had to sleep in a small entombed cellar branching off at the back of the first cellar. Entry was by a doorway, the top of which was often not higher than the level of the street.

Some of the occupants of the street cellars, nevertheless,

Canning Dock, c 1912
This crowded corner of the Canning Dock is filled with steam-powered vessels and Mersey Flats. The latter were the sail-powered barges used on the canals which led from the River Mersey. There crews, usually two men and perhaps a boy, were famous for their knowledge of the tides and other natural local sailing hazards. By the end of the 19th century many Flats had their sails removed and were towed by steam tugs

Wapping Dock, c 1906
The function of Wapping Dock as a linkage passage within the southern docks is illustrated in this postcard. Though many sailing ships have claimed a quayside berth alongside the storage transit sheds the dock passages are relatively clear. This branch style of narrow docks, affording lengthy quay spaces on both sides was part of Jesse Hartley's intention to increase communication within Liverpool's south docks. Ships like those shown could off-load in one dock and move on to another without having to return to the river to do so.

opened their homes for the sale of ale or whisky. Anyone entering these liquor cellars might typically see them to be about four yards square in size with tables and seats attached to each wall. They were frequented by drunken, foulmouthed men and women usually in the company of very young children.

Though the members of the watch committee became increasingly reluctant to allow Liverpool's policemen to persist with their public health duties each constable was instructed, in January 1848, to make a return of all the courts and cellars on his beat. Four constables, since 1846 in fact, had already been employed on a full-time basis for the health committee in this capacity.

Having originally been loaned for a fortnight these four men became exclusively devoted to the work of the health committee, and although the watch committee paid them, Head Constable Dowling was not allowed to interfere in their health work. More significantly, in January 1848, the health committee made six proposals to the watch committee. They urged that the police should be issued with lists of middens to be emptied at night and that they should report each morning whether they had been emptied; that they should report any nuisances, such as excessively smoking furnaces, cellars illegally occupied and overcrowding in the lodging houses; that they should also daily report broken flagstones, choked sewers or leaky gas pipes; that during heavy rainfall they should open sewer grids to release trapped surface water; that they should inspect the night watchmen of pavements and sewers; finally, that they should report any misconduct by street sweepers or water cart drivers.

In fact the police had carried out the last four proposals for many years but the watch committee finally decided, in 1848, that they should neither inspect the privies nor were they legally empowered to inspect the cellars nor enter the common lodging houses. Meanwhile, however, the four 'permanent men' continued to report on illegally used cellars.

In addition, during the cholera epidemic which swept through Liverpool, in 1849, the watch committee instructed the constables to give Dr. Duncan every assistance. These policemen worked in close cooperation with the various district medical officers, helping with, amongst other matters, the removal of the healthy or sick from those dwellings where the disease appeared to be most virulent. They also assisted with the speedy removal of the dead.

Perhaps, in view of the atrocious sanitary conditions that prevailed in the common lodging houses, in the courts and in the cellars it was not surprising that this water-borne disease broke out in epidemic proportions in Liverpool. The port's inadequate water supply had remained in private ownership until 1847 and vast numbers of people in the overcrowded districts had scant opportunity to cleanse themselves or their homes satisfactorily. The seaport had no public fountains, or pumps, no stand-pipes for street cleaning, and few cattle troughs. Indeed only three years earlier the whole population of the parish of Liverpool, upwards of 20,000 persons were found to be absolutely without any place of deposit for their refuse matter. Some 26 streets, in the early forties, moreover, between Scotland Road and Vauxhall Road and containing about 1,200 front houses, had 804, or two-thirds, without either yard, privy or ash-pit. Local people as a consequence deposited their filth in the corners of courts, in the entries, the back passages and even in the front streets.

Police officers, moreover, regularly received complaints that uncovered animal carcasses were carried in large numbers through the town. Others complained that butchers and many other inhabitants threw the offal and rubbish from their shops and houses into the street. With some streets littered with unswept animal manure and children even being left to play in pools of horse waste, conditions became rife for the contamination of the limited fresh water supply.

Three police sergeants were appointed in 1848 to disinfect, when necessary, the registered lodging houses but so many members of the police force were themselves attacked by cholera, falling ill initially with violent purgings and vomitings, that the Vauxhall bridewell, close to Vauxhall Road Infirmary had to be closed. The bridewell keeper and his family there eventually had to leave and take private lodgings.

One month later it was agreed that constables who fell

victims of the epidemic should be paid in full, upon being certified by the police surgeon. Despite the invaluable police help, however, the health committee still refused, in May 1850, to allow the free use of their public baths, such as those in Cornwallis Street, to those constables engaged in lodging house inspections.

Even the prisons' inspector reported a more active disease level between 1847 and 1848 in Kirkdale Gaol, with dysentry, scurvy, fever, influenza and typhus being prevalent particularly among the destitute Irish there. To guard against a cholera outbreak in the borough prison, in 1850, two temporary hospitals were set up, the great cesspool was filled in and human waste had to be carried beyond the prison grounds.

As the merchants improved their own prosperity the constables expected to be given greater responsibilities. They found this to be so, in 1858, for example, when additional recruits joined them to assist at Liverpool's new landing stage, at the Wapping warehouses and at the railway gates of the Waterloo and Sandon Docks.

Towards the end of the century the constables had increasingly to be on extra duty as the dockers became a more politically unified body of men. The police found themselves stretched to their limits for twenty-four days in February, 1879. On the first day of that month, gangs of dockers suddenly stormed into the docks, drove out strike blacklegs, and tipped the ships' gangways into the docks.

Major Greig, head constable, became so alarmed that he rode to the North Fort and demanded the help of a small company of militia. While the latter marched and stationed themselves at Collingwood Dock, a detachment of Dragoon Guards hid in a large shed at Clarence Dock. Yet a further three hundred infantrymen and seventy Dragoons came to help the police when the coal heavers and merchant seamen also joined the strikers. They all peacefully ended their strike on the 25th February, but the policemen stayed on alert for some days after.

The dockers had long realised that their problems stemmed from the everchanging tonnage of shipping in the docks. When the ships sailed and emptied some docks, the labourers joined a large pool of unemployed dockers. By the eighties, even though few of them worked for more than a few days each week, many in their ranks still did not favour starting a permanent pool of dockers since they realised the majority of them would be worse off than before.

The unionists again struck for improved wages and conditions in February and March, 1890. When 25,000 formed a procession, wearing their union buttons and accompanied by their bands, banners and flags, they marched through Liverpool's docklands and principal streets. Head Constable William Nott-Bower had to again request military aid. This time the soldiers marched into the docks and quartered on board some of the ships there. Finally, their presence, together with Michael Davitt's negotiations, as a labour leader, saw the men end their strike.

Within twelve months of their return to work, however, the dockers again were faced with most of their former problems. Their work was still dangerous, their hours were still irregular and the Employers Labour Association was still powerful enough to ban the union 'button' men. As a consequence the dockers' Merseyside membership declined from 15,000 to less than 6,000. Though some resorted to systematic go-slow practices and other shoddy working patterns it was probably the avoidance of a major dispute in the 1890's, that helped the men to re-develop the strength of their unions.

By 1902 their five Merseyside branches had the support of 9,500 members but up to one third of these were behind in the payment of their subscriptions. In Liverpool the characteristic differences, too, concerning 'shipmen' and porters persisted. The shipmen, the better paid of the two, loaded and unloaded vessels. The porters, for their part, enjoyed safer working conditions and arranged the cargoes on the quayside. The average employment for both groups of men, remained at three days per week and induced poverty on a large scale.

This vulnerability of the dockers to sporadic work continued along with the hazards of handling certain cargoes such as cement, bulk guano, bleaching powder, sulphur, pitch and hides. Long-term work as a docker, some medical opinion propounded, led to inevitable bodily disfigurement.

The replacement of sailing ships by steam vessels removed some of these problems but the main aim of the employers continued to be that ships be turned round as quickly as possible and that they did not lie idle. By 1906 their steam ships represented some 98 per cent of the port's traffic and their growing fleets of merchants steamers hastened the rapid decline of those docks such as the Albert Dock, catering principally for the sailing ships.

Brunswick Dock, c 1901
The use of steam tugs to tow sailing ships, as shown, began in the 1820's in Liverpool. Vessels, like the Invergarry, shown c 1901, could be efficiently taken from a quayside berth. When outward-bound, a sailing ship could be taken by steam tug beyond any dangerous river obstacles. By this means, too, ships could avoid being held up for several weeks by contrary winds.

5

Prisoners, Treadmills and Scouse

Any persons arrested in the docklands could expect to be dragged to the special lockups, or bridewells, like those at the Collingwood and Prince's docks. Adult and child thieves, together with drunkards, brothel-keepers, prostitutes and violent sailors would be treated alike and taken on foot there. Once convicted, by a magistrate or a sessions' judge, they might be chained and marched in fetters, or taken in a huge, covered horse-drawn van to serve their time in the nearby Howard Street Borough Gaol or to the County House of Correction at Kirkdale.

However, some of those taken to the dock bridewells were shown compassion by the dock constables. This was especially so if they had been injured or been in danger of drowning at the docks.

During one of the wildest storms on the River Mersey, in the winter of 1839, those dock constables on duty had to face scenes of awe and danger there. Liverpool people totally deserted the streets as showers of chimney bricks, slates and old walls fell around them. Many ships crashed into each other on the river, whilst others smashed down the pierheads and nearly all the boats and vessels in the basins crashed against the stone walls and sank. The

constables, meanwhile, had to patrol as far as Bootle Bay
to protect the damaged shipping from coastal wreckers.

On these occasions they worked magnificently using their
bridewell stretchers to carry the injured, or any
abandoned drunkards, to the safety of the nearest hospital
or receiving house. They often used their own bridewell,
such as those in the Collingwood and Prince's docks to
give aid to anyone who had fallen into the dock or river.

Those constables operating from the Collingwood station
in the fifties had the use of a large bath and a boiler which
was kept heated by both day and night so that any person
rescued from drowning could be given a warm bath on
arrival at the lockup. As soon as the constable entered the
bridewell with such a rescued party, a messenger was sent
by horse-drawn carriage to the Vauxhall dispensary for a
surgeon. Other dock policemen sent such cases, from
other bridewells, to the Prince's Dock station, or the
Southern Hospital.

These constables had enjoyed the use of superior lockup
houses compared to those of the town. For a fee, the
wealthier accused could usually be provided with a bed at
these bridewells. They were clean and well-ventilated,
and their cells were lit by gas light by night and contained
strong benches with coarse leather pillows.

After engaging in violent struggles, the constables knew
they would be able to take their most dangerous prisoners
and strap them to any of the special cast iron rings bolted

The Borough Gaol, Great Howard Street, 1856
The Gaol was situated in the heart of the docklands inshore from the Waterloo Dock.
In 1842 during the immensely destructive warehouse fires, in the Formby and
Neptune Street District, the Gaol itself was in danger of being consumed in the
flames. *From a photograph of a watercolour in the Herdman Collection.*

Emily Place, 1897
The tradition of court inhabitants in Liverpool congregating outside their homes is
clearly reflected in this photograph. The deplorable living conditions are evident in
the confined cellar dwelling entrances and the rubbish and dirt accumulating in the
muddy stretches of the unpaved sections of the courtyard.

to some of the cell walls there. Once inside, miscreants had to send out a message to their friends or relatives to supply them with food. If they did not, or if they were destitute, the police would supply them with only bread and water. Their life became worse, moreover, if they were sent to trial, were convicted and then sent to a Liverpool gaol.

To enter the nearby borough gaol was a woeful experience. The prisoners lived a lice-ridden and overcrowded existence there. They had to use makeshift toilets, workrooms, bedding and clothing in a gaol built in 1783, which in part had been utilised for prisoners during the Napoleonic Wars. After a few days even the women found themselves to be creeping alive with vermin, because they could not bathe, launder or disinfect themselves when inside. Much of the gaol, in fact, had remained unoccupied from the end of the wars against France until 1836. Yet for six months in 1833, when the cholera epidemic raged, prisoners who should have been committed to the infected Kirkdale County Prison entered there instead. Women and men alike, sent to the borough gaol, also, commonly complained of being afflicted with gonorrhoea and syphilis.

Those prisoners sent to the Kirkdale Correction House, by comparison, might have initially felt themselves to be luckier. The gaol had been constructed on a noble, elevated site, commanding a fine open view of the River Mersey. Once inside, however, they were condemned to a brutalising way of life. Children, like the adults, could be fettered in the solitary cells. Their visitors had to travel about two miles from the Liverpool Exchange if they came from the centre of the borough. Then they would have to force themselves past the throngs of vile characters who hung around the prison gates both by night and day. Inside, convicts could expect better ventilated and better drained cells than those in Great Howard Street but the men and boys found their quarters terribly overcrowded. They found this to be the case, too, when they used the exercise yards, the workshops, (including a tin shop and a joiners' shop) the schoolroom and the kitchen.

All the seaport's prisoners soon realised that life inside prison was harsh and degrading. Immediately they entered through the prison gates they had their personal property and clothing stripped from them. The men and boys each had to collect an ill-fitting jacket, a cap, trousers, a shirt, a pair of well-used clogs and a coarse woollen shirt for nightwear. Then they were further branded by the colour coding of their prison clothing. For a minor offence the prisoners could expect a blue marking. Felons known to have only one previous conviction received grey and yellow. Any who needed to be recognised as having served several sentences in prison received red and blue.

Female prisoners, both girls and women, could expect little better. On entering they had to accept a day and a night headcap, a cotton and flannel petticoat, a long shift and a linen bedgown. All prisoners knew that ahead of them was hard, daily labour, whereby they had to work on the treadmills, the crank handle machines for raising water from ground-level to the loft tanks and even stone breaking. If they became truculent they knew that they would be forced to pick oakum in silence.

None could expect any change from their monotonous daily routines. This was especially so in their cycle of inadequate meals. They faced a breakfast similar to supper, consisting of a pint of gruel and half a pound of bread. At their other daily meal, a dinner, they queued for either scouse, or cow-head broth and a half pound of bread, or perhaps for two ounces of bacon and half a pound of potatoes.

In time the prisoners swelled their numbers so greatly they became unmanageable in the port's two old gaols. More and more came to be driven into criminal acts by their own desperate circumstances. Numerous Irish immigrants, men, women and children alike, found themselves committed to prison life in the depression years of the forties. Captain Williams, the experienced Northern District Prison Inspector wrote of them in 1847:

"the increase in prisoners is almost entirely of Irish prisoners, November, December and January (the Winter months) were heaviest, particularly for vagrancy and pilferings, some with the express object of getting into prison."

Such unfortunates generally committed their crimes when they found themselves spurred on by destitution, knowing that if they applied for parish poor relief, under the alteration of the law of settlement, they would have been sent back to famine stricken Ireland. Kirkdale Gaol's governor supported the inspector in his views and felt their drunkenness, their lack of education, their failure in the trade depression to find work and their consequent destitution had caused a high tide of criminal activity.

Such officials, however, hoped that Liverpool prisoners would face the prospect of improved prison life when the old gaols were closed and replaced by the new, well constructed Walton Gaol. Visiting dignitaries, on opening day in 1855 felt it would be well served by its twenty-three acres of ground and its thousand cells and they felt that the cost to the Liverpool Corporation of about £180,000 was well justified. Within three years of being opened, however, many believed it to be inadequate because of the many extra dock and town criminals arriving there.

Both male and female convicts moved into their separated quarters once inside it. The hardest form of labour was to work the gaol treadwheel or help turn one of the twelve cranks used to raise water from the wells to the gaol's cisterns. Those prisoners in need of extreme punishment could expect to be placed in solitary confinement in one of the thirty, dark basement cells or punished by the lash on the whipping frame. Fortunately, the majority of prisoners only entered gaol, at first, for a short term. In 1857 about three-quarters of the men entering the gaol were to serve less than one month inside.

6

Drunkards on the Dock Road

Many of those who lived at, or near the Liverpool Docks in the eighteen thirties and forties, lived raw and degrading lives. Liverpool drunkards, sailors' girls and young lawbreakers plagued them and pestered any visitor who came into contact with them. Even the most honest and hardworking dock labourers usually found it necessary to search for employment in this region by going into the public houses that stretched along the likes of Regent Road, Bath Street and Waterloo Road. These became collectively known to local people as the Dock Road. Thus those seeking to employ consistently well-behaved labourers for the Albert and other docks would have found it difficult to do so.

John Finch, a Liverpool social pioneer and a founder of the Liverpool Temperance Society, believed the dock labourers to be the Liverpudlians who drank in the heaviest fashion. In 1834, he blamed the lumpers, the men who received an agreed lump sum for the job of finding labourers to load or discharge the numerous cargoes, for the dockers' plight. The lumpers, he discovered, went to the quaysides to recruit the dockers and they made a considerable profit by taking on the men at much less than the price they agreed with the merchants. On one occasion, Finch found out that of 120 men to be recruited in this way, only a few had not been paid off in a dockside public house.

In practice, if the dockers did not meet and drink regularly in certain Dock Road and dock district pubs, they had little chance of getting any work. The areas in from New Quay, Bath Street and Waterloo Road offered a host of low class drinking dens. At the centre of the port favourite public houses included the Crows Nest, the Steer-in, Murphys Saloon, the Dewdrop, and Devine's Hotel. In the Wapping district (close to the Albert Dock) the Baltic Fleet, which still stands, became well patronised, as does another further north on the Dock Road, the A1 at Lloyds.

Gatherings of lumpers and dock labourers reputedly drank gallons of fourpenny ale in any drinking session. Sunday became a popular day to drink, with a host of waiters, some wearing their distinctive pork pie hats, 'waiting on' as many as four to a bar. In some instances father, shawl-wrapped mother, children and grand-children joined together as glass upon glass from a large half-gallon jug was poured out and passed around.

In the likes of Charles Street and district many families made collections amongst themselves and often sent out to the beershops for jugs of ale to take home and drink in a chosen court house. Sometimes, amid the gathered groups of the families, brawling inevitably broke out. It was not unknown for a half-gallon jug to be used in passion by a jealous wife to separate her husband, by blows, from a neighbour's wife's attentions. Such outbursts in turn sometimes even sparked full scale street riots.

Whilst beerhouses such as those in Charles Street, Chisenhale Street and other similar streets became notorious for those who easily fell into violence, lumpers and dockers alike also took drink in the gambling stalls or shops, such as those near the Sailors' Home. In such they had the opportunity, after liquor, to wager their entire wages on the wheels-of-fortune or the gambling tables therein.

Workers not of the poorest grade, such as the lumpers, also visited the infamous card playing houses in these districts. Many used the slate, or credit facility, often leaving with a debt of as much as fourteen shillings after any one visit. Police knew of many such licensed gambling houses at this time near the docks. In one such beerhouse, for example, they knew of dockers regularly playing cards and being induced, week after week, to languish there, often spending all their wages and in turn making their families almost permanently destitute.

At another establishment, occupying a prominent position in town, men of all classes of society, including those from the docks, went to smoke cigars, sip brandy and chat with degraded girls. Others studied the scantily dressed 'living tableaux', or joined in with the filthiest of songs, such as

The Lively Flea, which they usually accompanied with the vilest of actions.

Hence John Finch, together with many of his reforming associates, brought his energies so fully against the boozing dens that he became known as the King of the Teetotalers. He became particularly appalled when he saw thousands of decent but wretchedly clothed and badly fed dockers and warehouse men forever hanging around the quaysides.

They even had to wait in the worst of weather, hoping that the lumpers would eventually emerge from the public houses. Those lucky enough to work in the thirties collected a wage of two shillings a day for their, at best, three or four day week.

With the help of men like Finch and some of the more benevolent merchants, such as the Rathbone brothers, thousands of dockers and warehouse men managed to join a cooperative society which fixed their wages at three shillings. In doing without the middlemen, the individual docker found himself able to raise his wages by half. Torn by their religious bigotry and political differences, however, and in the face of a continuing influx of 'free' labourers from beyond Liverpool, they gradually fell into disunity and caused their own cooperative to collapse. Perhaps the lumpers, therefore, did not always deserve the vitriolic criticism cast upon them by the strongminded reformers such as John Finch and his associates. In 1839, the Head Constable of Liverpool, Michael Whitty, investigated a series of accusations made against those lumpers working at the Prince's Dock.

After conducting a very strict inquiry into their operations he found that they had acted in a perfectly legal manner and that they were also peacefully disposed men. In fact it was the lumpers who had been annoyed and assaulted by by a set of men belonging to another club, or association, who went about the docks trying to prevent those dockers from working who did not belong to their club. Whitty, moreover, regarded the lumpers' union as greatly having helped in changing their men's conduct so much so that the dock policemen believed the lumpers had 'recently wonderfully improved as to honesty and sobriety'.

Nevertheless, some of the temperance-minded followers made their own sustained attempt to persuade the dock labourers to stop their heavy bouts of drinking. A small dedicated group of young men began to meet in a dockside coffee house in Greenland Street, between James Street and Chaloner Street, and they eventually formed a temperance missionary society. On Sundays they visited the working class districts of Liverpool and even entered those which they knew the police had become reluctant to enter. By 1839, their temperance movement had swelled to support as many as fourteen Liverpool Societies.

This groundswell of support had been significantly inspired by the revulsion of the torrent of liquor flowing through the seaport after the Beer Bill of 1830. By this, any person who had his name on the ratebook could be induced to open his home as a beershop, free from licensing control, if he was able to find the necessary two guineas demanded at the local excise office. Some 800 Liverpudlians opened their houses in this way in the first eighteen days after the Act. By such enthusiasm they gave Liverpool more pubs, in proportion to the people living there, than any other large town in Victoria's realm, excluding the city of London.

In time the beershop operators tranferred their rights to anyone who would buy them. Many such purchasers added to their income by inviting prostitutes into their premises. Some of the latter were those girls who were known to have been seduced from their own homes, or from working as respectable family servants, by madams, or women brothelminders. The madams often posed as washer women and entered the household in disguise. The police knew many respectable girls who had fallen into their traps having been lured to the waterfront by tales of glamour or the amusements they could enjoy in Liverpool.

In reality the beershops and other sources of drink, such as the grogshops, whisky, and pennyale cellars, eventually stretched their tentacles into that formidable section of the port where dockers, warehousemen, sailors, emigrants and the like came to stay.

Dock labourers, carters and other similar men together with the families of the roughest and humblest class settled in the likes of Vauxhall Road and in all its adjacent streets. Weather permitting they sat out till two or three o'clock, or later, on warm Sunday mornings. They contrasted with those living in the Marybone district, where men often earned a living in the nearby countryside, returning home late on Saturdays but making their district drinking dens more uproarious on Sunday nights and Monday mornings.

In this period Scotland Road teemed with moving throngs, such as the rowdy little lads with their short pipes in their mouths. They in turn conversed with young girls, 'Cyprian in modesty and utterly brutal in demeanour and conversation'. Here, for a halfpenny they could listen to street singers selling details of recent brutal murders or dreadful accidents. Similar characters might be met in Ashton Street, in the Toxteth Park district, where dirty unshaven labourers sat without coats and shoes on the steps of their courthouses watching swarms of children playing hopscotch, or imitating local funeral processions, or the activities of carters. The women, too, watched in their tattered dresses. Such occupants usually sat unmoved as the children played in the unpaved, unflagged streets strewn with decaying matter, horse manure and other garbage.

Bolton Street, Croston Street and Glover Street also harboured similar wretched conditions. The latter became the resort of half-naked, lewd men and women, carters and ruffians and was a narrow street, about 100 yards long. Some decent artisans, however, did strive to improve even the humblest of such districts. Back Grafton

Street, Wolfe Street and Henderson Street, for example, were generally neat compared to the likes of Upper Mann Street which had horrifying courts and cellars. South Park Street, too, contained a very good class of house but lacked paving and like many others developed deep cartwheel ruts and large holes at times filled with stagnant water.

Many such districts, became characterised by their thick, smoke-filled and foul-vapoured atmosphere. Some beer houses in these districts welcomed gaudily-dressed girls sometimes in the company of half-dressed labouring men. In the Vauxhall Road and Leeds Street beerhouses the notorious 'Liverpool roughs' became a common sight. These apparently became characterised by their short stature, large heads, broad flat faces and thick necks. Such ruffians turned up their white trouser bottoms to reveal their high-laced greasy boots. In Banastre Street such louts, some in the company of brutalized women with black eyes, or cuts on their cheeks or forehead, lay across the doorway entrances into the spirit vaults.

Several even more notorious beerhouses became the haunts of various visiting sailors. American coloured seamen met in throngs at the Kentucky Vaults beerhouse in Scotland Road. Here, they surrounded the bars dressed in 'superfine coats of the fastest cut, linen of snowy whiteness of the most flashy pattern, rings upon their fingers, and shirt studs of the greatest lustre and most enormous size'. They crowded into the lobbies in such numbers that it was almost impossible to move past them.

However, once through, into the kitchen and up a set of rickety stairs, patrons could enter the ballroom, lit by a single jet, and join a quadrille with young white girl dancers.

Throngs of emigrants, too, received directions to enter this district, via Chisenhale Street and its canal bridge, for it formed a direct thoroughfare with the docks. Unfortunately, in the fifties, it became plagued by a gang of ruffians who carried out a series of violent robberies. Sometimes they even heaved their victims into the canal. Another additional snare in this vicinity, too, was an infamous brothel in one of the back court houses. Here sailors arriving by carriage from the docks might be met by women in a state of undress.

Liverpool policemen, in time, reported hundreds of known prostitutes and infamous thieves who ran such drinking dens. They also confronted the prostitutes as they plied for trade in the cheap dockside singing saloons. In these, numerous young boys and girls fell into depravity of every type when under the spell of the notorious coarse dancers and singers there. In time, many hundreds of children came to frequent such places being seen there at any time of the day or night when they smoked, drank liquor and saturated themselves in the most degrading ribaldry and obscenity.

Many respectable persons, and these included some of the dock constables who sought to put an end to such sources of drinking, were often viciously threatened by the brewers and spirit merchants. Some of the latter were even reputed to have served on the Liverpool Watch Committee. Such powerful brewers naturally did all they could to protect their liquor outlets.

They especially tried to frustrate the hated plain clothes policemen who began to operate more systematically towards the middle of the century. At one point, Head Constable John Greig (1852-1881), received instructions to forbid his men using any spying techniques. He ordered them not to keyhole peep, climb over walls into private property, or dress up in coalheaver or dock labourer disguises.

Fortunately, Liverpudlians became more temperate in their drinking habits, but it was not until many decades of gradual amelioration in their social conditions had helped them to do so. The principal efforts to help the poorer areas came mainly from the members of the Temperance Movement. The Liverpool based enthusiasts in this field embarked on several noteworthy improvements. These took the form of The Police Court and Prison Gate Mission which, after its inauguration in 1879, contacted many thousands of local people annually. Other smaller developments included the Women's Shelter 1887, and The Church of England Temperance Society's Firwood and Mat Factory, 1891.

The approach of these organisations contrasted starkly with the more direct methods of those who sought to restrict licensing hours by legislation. Instead of the patient social reconstruction of the temperance reformers the more radical advocates of parliamentary intervention demanded statutes such as the 1872 Liquor Licensing Act which noticeably limited the time publicans could keep open their premises. Such a drastic approach, restricting opening hours to between 7am. and 11pm. merely served to encourage bootlegging activities and the growth of illicit stills.

That some other more subtle approach was required may be seen in the fact that though some 12,000 drunkards were apprehended in the seaport in 1874 only three licensees were found to be guilty of liquor offences. In this year an aggregate of 1,929 public houses, 383 beerhouses and 272 off-licences and refreshment houses provided a vast number of liquor outlets. Many ordinary constables on a cold winter's night, it was reported, found it difficult to resist these forms of temptation 'when liquor is held to their lips'. For the average citizen the legitimate sources of alcohol outnumbered all their local grocery, furniture, chemist and stationery shops.

Some of the most celebrated visitors to the port had to confront this dark side of life in Liverpool. P. J. Waller has admirably researched and depicted how novelists or poets, like Hugh Walpole and Gerard Manley Hopkins, found this to be so. Charles Dickens recorded some of his pleasant experiences in Liverpool but he also had to come to terms with those less savoury aspects of his visits. After corporation officials honoured him in St. George's Hall with a banquet, a drunken cloakroom brawl between dignitaries occurred to mar its end.

As seen above, such intemperance appears to have become endemic over several decades and was particularly rife amongst the youngest of persons. In 1876 some 352 of the drunks convicted were aged under twelve; and some 1,525 were aged from twelve to eighteen. These were the best returns of the 1870s and for many years much social reform was needed to improve matters.

Even after twenty years of national education it was reported that the only clock that many Liverpudlians knew was 'the closing hours of the public houses'. Well after the end of the hey-day of the sailing ship in the south docks the struggle against excessive drinking was set to continue.

Beershop patrons, c 1890
The practice of sending children for jugs of ale persisted over many decades in Liverpool. This official police photograph, c 1890, shows two infants in the vicinity of a beershop. Amongst the signs in the background is one for 'Half and Half', or bitter ale mixed with mild.

7

Riverside Urchins

Of all the shameful behaviour, at or near the Liverpool docks, that of the thousands of desperate boys and girls was most hurtful to respectable Liverpool folk. Gangs of these ill-clad, ill-fed and usually homeless urchins roamed the streets, alleyways and entries of the noisy seaport.

Many abandoned their wretched slum homes after stealing pennies from a shelf, a drawer, or from their drunken parents to join their friends in some low singing saloon or theatre. Their late hours, wicked friendships, home desertion and theft from shops led them quickly into becoming riverside vagabonds.

One of the most hardened prison inspectors, Captain Williams, painfully admitted, in 1841, that he believed that more young criminals lived in Liverpool than in any other of the great manufacturing or commercial centres in Queen Victoria's realm, including Metropolitan London.

These Liverpool youngsters also seemed to show greater desperation than the adult criminals. A short walk from the Albert Dock, or from the adjoining Canning or Salthouse docks, would bring any visiting sailor face to face with the most notorious characters and their haunts around Canning Place and the Sailors'Home.

Walking from the Home along the cobble-stoned Coopers Row and on into Paradise Street, they could enter the likes of Hood Street in a matter of minutes. On such a walk, Captain Williams himself passed many low theatres and bawdy places of amusement. He felt the Sanspareil, the Liver, the Queen's Theatre, the Custom House, the Hood Street Penny Hop and many others there, to be among the worst he had ever seen. Young boys gathered in throngs in these streets, hoping to see some of those performances put on two or three times each night. Shoeless and stockingless boys and girls alike, entered the Hop through a dark passageway in Hood Street and climbed a ladder staircase to enter the crude theatre room which was fitted out in the roughest fashion.

Once they passed beyond the gaudily painted fronts of such places, they eagerly waited to see the actors portay horrific scenes of crime and bloodshed. Their Liverpool 'favourites' showed them the obscene murder of Maria Martin in the Red Barn, or of Hannah Brown by Greenacre. Indeed, they enjoyed any vile atrocities on offer. Some theatre managers even dramatically presented in their plays types of schools for thieves, with a host of villainous lessons.

At the time Prince Albert visited the Liverpool docklands, many rogue managers had such scenes playing to packed houses in their sleazy theatres. Hugh Shimmin, a

dependable Liverpool newspaper reporter, was appalled
by such depravity in the fifties. On one occasion he saw
three young men being thrown out of an old stable that
stood on the corner of Roe Street and Lime Street.
Intrigued, he entered. This was advertised as that of a
"medical galvanist open for scientific and instructive
entertainment, embracing Sir Hugh Davy's nitrous oxide
and other laughable experiments." Boys and girls used
the apparatus on themselves and grimaced and twisted in
pain as a result.

Others behaved equally disgustingly, using shameful and
obscene language. At yet another place, Shimmin, saw a
woman suckling an infant as she sat on an outside bench
which she shared with a voluptuous woman of known
easy virtue. Both women, moreover, showed themselves
to be half asleep, and near drunk.

Any jack tar, paid off at the port, could quickly travel on
foot, or by cab if drunk, to the heart of the city. Seeking
out their favourite haunts, they could enter the
Williamson Square Free Concert Room, or the Nelson
Street concert, or gambling halls. In some they might risk
their lives as was the case when they went into the
dilapidated converted warehouse which they knew as
The Royal Casino. Still others might opt for the Salle de
Danse Theatre to wager on the battered-faced, bare-fisted
fighters or on the fighting-dog battles.

Many of the younger visitors became thieves when they
saw the vast amount of unguarded property around the

dock and quaysides. Thousands of shopkeepers, dock warehouse labourers, street and market traders carelessly left out goods of all types such as ropes, trousers, waistcoats and stockings, cuts of beef and ham, and bagged or loose sugar. Those who nimbly snatched any valuables knew they would be able to sell them quickly to any of the known receivers of stolen property or to any of the pawnbrokers.

Those desperate children who found themselves caught and arrested for pick-pocketing, or for simply stealing food like pies and cabbages to eat, were taken to the bridewells and later to the gaols. After release most usually returned to their old vagabond way of life. The young Liverpool boys became particularly notorious at the docks by day for stealing ropes, copper and marine stores of every type. By night, they deserted the docks to exchange their stolen goods in the brothels, rookeries or flash houses, and then went on to visit their amusement fleshpots. After their night of entertainment they would seek out a place to sleep in. They regularly resorted to using a deserted stable, a coach or a carriage. Some even found their way into the vaults and cellars of public houses, or into a pig-sty or a disease-ridden privy.

Irish immigrant children were particularly known to behave in this way, as many found themselves stranded in Liverpool when their parents died from cholera or fever. These and other children became hardened law-breakers and went on to steal from washing lines, or shops, and even delighted in hurling stones at respectable

Liverpool citizens as they came out of church on Sunday. Such children and the very youngest members of their family often fell into the clutches of the chimney sweeps or became servants of local infamous baby farmers.

Many Liverpool children, hardened by such a dreadful existence, became obstinate and unrepentant after enduring their cruel prison life. Extremely wayward ones had to face up to transportation. Some of the local prison chaplains blamed the horrifying conditions in the borough and Kirkdale gaols for worsening even the most difficult boys and asking that a separate asylum be set aside in Liverpool to receive them. Members of the Liverpool Corporation moved in their own way, in 1840, and directed that funds be granted for apprenticing such boys to the captains of vessels bound for the British colonies.

Perhaps the most desperate groups of children were those who lived in the dockland districts near the Salthouse Dock, in James Street, or those in the districts stretching up from the North Shore to Scotland Road. As many as 30,000 Liverpool children, about half the number living in the port in the thirties, received no education whatsoever. Others did visit some schools but in these they sat in confined, damp and dirty places, often falling ill with measles, scarlet fever, smallpox and eye infections. Almost forty years later some Liverpool children still had to face similar appalling conditions when they found they could be compelled to attend school.

Some did escape from life in prison by being sent to serve their sentence in a reformatory. They would be taken to farms, or vessels like the Clarence or Akbar, anchored in the River Mersey. Such children could have their parents compelled to pay toward their upkeep.

Several merchants and shipowners became staggered by the swarms of delinquent boys they saw infesting the docks with their crimes. They formed a committee and had the Akbar hulk fitted out as a training school and moved into the centre of the Birkenhead Large Float. Any offending boy could then be sent to Birkenhead and out to the Akbar by way of a small rowing boat which was under the command of a well known ruddy-faced boatswain and six young oarsmen.

They and their shipmates, as many as 150 boys, kept the hulk in excellent order. Once aboard they found a superintendent, a schoolmaster, the boatswain and his mate, a purser, a steward, a carpenter, a cook and two other seamen living there. These men disciplined the boys and expected them to share the watch at special points, such as aloft in the foresail, or in the maintop. The boys, in turn, had their own junior captain and had their duties methodically listed so that they could be traced at any time of the night or day. Using the books of the Irish Society, they attended school for up to three hours each day.

They ate amidships, in naval fashion, close to the modern style galley. They ate well, too, their junks of beef contrasting with the bacon scraps or scouse of gaol prisoners. Nor did they see anything to remind them of prison. After sleeping in the lower deck dormitory they would roll up their hammocks and place them neatly in the centre of the deck floor next to their large numberd, personal kitbags. In their bags they kept a change of clothing. When ill, they could visit the hospital adjoining their lower deck dormitory.

Thankfully, by 1870, as the reformatories and School Board helped such children to become more purposefully occupied, the number of those engaged in larceny began to fall. Some still, however, sought to engage in criminal activities, like those in the infamous professional thieves' schools. Some entered the notorious one in the Upper Canada district near the Rose Hill bridewell. In such places, boys and girls still regularly trained in the graded skills of simple pick-pocketing or grand larceny. These thieves' colleges had Fagin-type professors who spent much of their daily life in the police courts studying the mistakes of those who came before the magistrates.

Nevertheless, many children when brutally beaten by adults, or living in poverty or misery, took to seeking a livelihood by begging, or hawking, in the dockland streets. As late as 1898, numerous Liverpool children hawked in the streets, particularly when they obtained a licence to do so. Only a few years earlier as many as 4,500 children, found wandering in the Liverpool districts, were seen to be insufficiently clothed and destitute. Those children living in the docklands, also, became recognisable as the poorest and those most obviously suffering from unemployment, drunkenness and the violence of seaport life.

Bare Feet Days, c 1890
Two Liverpool women, one with traditional shoulder shawl and the other with apron and in bare feet, engage in conversation. In the background, on the right, another sits on the doorway steps near the cellar entrances. The little girl in the foreground appears to be carrying a quart jug for beer from a local source.

8

Sailors' Girls

Few travellers who walked through the Liverpool docklands would be unaware of their evil reputation. Those engaged in violence, especially in stabbing incidents, gave the riverfront a deserved notoriety by the time His Royal Highness, Prince Albert, opened the famous dock. Until the middle of the sixties the majority of visiting sailors carried sheath daggers and constantly began drunken brawls and fits of fighting.

They came relentlessly, in the thirties, forties, fifties and sixties, from many other world famous seaports. Clipper seamen from North America, Liverpool Irish packet rats, China birds and West Indian and West African negroes and the like, flocked in and rubbed shoulders with each other in and around the docks.

Once outside the docks, the mariners stepped into the company of foul smelling and raggedly dressed, begging children, sailors' girls and lodging house touts. Requiring a place to rest from their dangerous voyages, the sailors quickly accepted the touts' offers of quarters near the riverfront. At first they swarmed into the lodgings in the South End district, in Canning Place, Paradise Street, Park Lane, Cleveland Square, Frederick Street and on into Park

Lane. They brought their own distinctive cargo, language, dress and behaviour and created a dramatic atmosphere of expectancy in the side streets, alleys and small courts there.

Others took their quarters in Castle Street, Derby Square, near the pierheads in New Quay and Waterloo Road districts. Coming ashore from the likes of Prince's and Waterloo docks, they met the locals who popularised this this area as the North End.

In time, they made most of these dock haunts swarm with loose women. In 1836, thousands of these girls regularly set out from the three hundred popular dockland and town brothels. These gaudily dressed women plied for their trade by systematically seeking out the sailor boys. Many also became expert in attracting seafarers of a particular nationality into their haunts. In the thirties, for example, North American seamen appear to have been lured into the Prince's Dock surrounds. After their danger-ridden existence on the high seas these men entered into a life of relative comfort ashore in Liverpool. Thus they impressed on each other the need to seek out the likes of the Baltimore Clipper tavern, in Union Street, as a place for relaxation.

Their lady friends became accepted members of the distinctive strand of shady dockside characters who helped to exploit the brashness of these seamy quarters. They worked alongside the local owners of the low theatres, singing saloons and fairgrounds, to supply cheap and sensuous relaxations. Some even sought out young boys and girls and kept houses for them to live together promiscuously. Others readily offered depraved entertainment on demand and included dog fighting as well as rat and badger baiting in their list of additional attractions.

Many girls, in turn, became exploited by others, such as the profiteers in the drinking trade. These became only too eager to supplement their income by letting 'Maggie Mays', or sailors' girls, use their premises. Members of Liverpool Corporation, in 1837, estimated that together, these girls earned as much as £734,240 in their notorious public brothels and their private lodgings.

Young girls travelled in their hundreds to Liverpool from other parts of Great Britain. Some, faced with hunger, sought, voluntarily, to go on the streets. With so relatively few respectable jobs for females, even by 1865, the friendless or destitute girl readily stepped into the seedy quarters looking for customers. Young Irish immigrant girls often found the need to sell themselves in this manner.

They knew they could only face arrest if they openly annoyed the respectable public. In most court cases, the brothel-keeper would have to face charges for keeping a disorderly house. More and more girls also took to the Liverpool streets as they became aware that provisions such as those in the 1864 Contagious Diseases Act did not apply to the likes of Liverpool girls, but to those in the garrison towns, where soldiers, not sailors, sought them out. Police constables in the seaport found that though known Liverpool girls of easy virtue increased from 686, in 1861 to 764 ten years later, they had nevertheless greatly reduced their numbers from the thirties.

Charitable Liverpool ladies from the wealthier families formed various societies to help such local girls whom they believed often suffered needlessly. By 1868, they knew such females could not find any Liverpool hospital that would treat them when infected with venereal disease. Some tramped up to the forbidding workhouse at the top of Brownlow Hill in desperation. Once there they would be turned away at the entrance, or thrown out of the lock wards, either because they were found to have the disease or because they could not show themselves to be destitute.

A few of the wealthier ones did manage to pay for their admission, by private subscription ticket, to the lock hospital connected to the Royal Infirmary. Most, however, found they would be left to suffer and spread their illness and had to accept mental collapse and eventual death. Those females following this calling and known to the police seem to have further reduced their numbers, from 1870-89, after some outrageous purges urged by local politicians. They reduced the numbers of brothel-keepers known in the port but drove the more casual and more shameless women to use the riverfront lodging houses, entries, alleyways and other public places to satisfy their clients.

Significant social problems associated with prostitution were to remain even by the end of the century. Large numbers of sailors continued to visit the seaport in steam-powered ships and many of them knew of and welcomed Liverpool's notoriety in such matters. A pamphlet 'The Deadly Shame of Liverpool', published in 1890, by Richard Armstrong, had accused the liquor trade of encouraging widespread prostitution. There was little evidence for some decades after the pamphlet's publication to indicate that matters had radically changed. At the same time the plight of venereal disease sufferers continued to be desperate. Medical advances improved after 1905 but it was not until 1916 that the Corporation Hospitals' Committee became obliged to render treatment in such cases.

Queen's Dock, c 1898
These splendid looking sailing ships are safely moored having been towed to the quayside by Mersey steam tugs. The vessels such as the Wiscombe Park, Caernarvon Bay and Gladowa are clearly identified. The clear central passageway of dock water complied with the intention of Jesse Hartley, the dock engineer, to operate an efficient 'turn round system'. Once the ships had entered the docks from the River Mersey the central passageway was kept clear so that outward-bound vessels could leave when required to do so.

9

River Policemen

When the Albert Dock was constructed in the great days
of the sailing ship, there was a heavy demand from
several sources that law and order should be as effectively
enforced on the River Mersey as it was on the Liverpool
quaysides. It was only after many years of disturbances on
the river that Mersey Docks and Harbour Board offered to
pay for an entirely new group of law enforcers. These
were known collectively as the Liverpool River Police and
they began their duties in June, 1865.

A superintendent of police, M. A. Seventy, formerly of the
Indian navy, led his men to parade at the town hall, in
Castle Street, in their own distinctive uniforms on the
inaugural day. The superintendent, three coxswains and
eighteen constables having received their basic uniform of
cap with badge, coat, trousers, souwester and guernsey
smock for river use, went out on patrol. On the river and
its docks and shores they used three gigs, or six-oared
boats, a re-call flag, a signal book, 'Maryalls' and for tidal
information a daily copy of the Liverpool Telegraph. They
suffered greatly, however, with at least one drowning,
when the Mersey Docks and Harbour Board insisted that
they should not be provided with a steam-powered
vessel. The men found their duties to be especially

Liverpool River Police, c 1897
The full complement of the Liverpool City River Police Department appears to be present in this remarkable photograph. These powerful looking policemen bravely patrolled the River Mersey using only small 'gigs', or rowing boats capable of carrying small sails from 1865-1899. Their original main duty was to prevent shanghaing or crimping.

Angleterre – Liverpool: Les Docks Saint-Georges, c 1895
This unusual postcard with French language caption, captures the cosmopolitan flavour of the Liverpool waterfront, c 1895. Steam and sail-powered vessels are shown crowded into this dock famous for its Mediterranean fruit trade in Victorian times. The continental origin of this photograph helps to illustrate Liverpool's international standing amongst the European sailing commuties. In the 1860's magistrates in the seaport had issued notices in seven languages in an attempt to reduce the number of violent assaults amongst visiting sailors.

dangerous at night when many steamers moved about in darkness on the river. They also often had to row amongst these vessels facing tides in excess of six miles per hour.

Members of the MDHB were forced to finance a river police department after the vessel 'Lotty Sleigh', with eleven tons of gun powder aboard, exploded whilst in the Sloyne in 1864. Property on both sides of the River Mersey, as a result, was greatly destroyed. In 1866, therefore, the MDHB instructed the men in the department to enforce the new bye-laws regarding the shipment of gun powder on the river.

The board recognised, however, that the river policemen should primarily curtail the activities of the crimps, or shanghaiers, on the river, at the pierheads and in the Sailors' Home, Canning Place.

The 'Liverpool Sailors' Home, Registry and Bank' was intended by its original trustees – a group of local benevolent gentlemen – to be a bastion against the ignorance and imprudence that prevailed amongst visiting seamen. A large number of sailors, they believed became victims of the corrupt Liverpool lodging house keepers. The trustees felt that such victims would in turn welcome the comfort and facilities provided by the well-regulated Home.

For their part the sailors had to provide a certificate of good character from their last employer. The men's needs, paid for by a moderate charge, were catered for, in the form of dining rooms, a reading room, religious instruction if requested, a library and a savings bank. Other features included dormitories, sufficient to accommodate 300 men, large kitchens, sculleries, a stewards room, pantries, a bakehouse, a beer cellar and eight sailors' chest rooms.

His Royal Highness, Prince Albert, laid the foundation stone for this fine building, Friday July 31, 1846 – the day after he opened the Albert Dock. Situated near to the Post Office, the Custom House and the central docks, the Home was built internally and externally, in a distinctive Elizabethan style. In time, Liverpool river police constables were to advise visiting sailors to take up residence there.

Such helpful assistance was aimed at protecting overseas mariners from moral, physical and pecuniary disaster. What is more it was indeed necessary, as Liverpool boasted the dubious reputation of 'the most immoral of all immoral places', and this notoriety owed much to the hosts of pimps, prostitutes and crimps who infested the Canning Place and Albert Dock districts. Many of these persons operated from the forty-six drinking dens which stood within a 200-yard radius of the Home in the 1870's and 1880's. In the nearby streets and doorways, encircled by these iniquitous liquor outlets extortionists, protection racketeers and pavement bookmakers sought to claim their own territory. Such ruthless recidivists became a constant threat to even the most dedicated of river policemen as well as to the sailors on shore leave.

The policemen also had to help the master of any vessel when he faced mutineers or an outbreak of fire. Indeed they had to protect any seafarer who asked for their help and they had to safeguard all the traffic passing to or from the ships, or those persons travelling between the docks, or shores on either side of the River Mersey.

Thus these river policemen began to exercise an authority that had been previously denied to officers in the force. Hitherto, their fellow constables had no legal power to board vessels, unless enforcing those bye-laws regarding the use of fires or lamps on board, or unless the Collector of Customs gave them power to board a ship. In fact their superiors, the watch committee, had previously discouraged them from working on the river believing that their duties on land demanded their full attention and it was unfair to have them perform duties that made unlawful financial demands on the ratepayers of Liverpool. Thus the constables themselves had up to this time been mainly content to pick up rewards for assisting the customs officers in collecting their dues.

Many dock constables had formerly felt incapable of considering river duty since dock duty itself was extremely difficult. To restrain refactory prisoners and to take them on foot to the nearest bridewell was often impossible. Such constables regularly confronted violent gangs of 'duffers', haranguing relatives of prisoners, or drunken sailors carrying sheath knives. One constable, for example, instantly bled to death, in November 1853, when stabbed in the femoral artery. In this year alone the magistrates dealt with 179 stabbing cases. By the early sixties, furthermore, visiting sailors had become involved in so many notorious knifing incidents on Liverpool's waterfront that the magistrates had issued notices in 7 different languages to deter sailors from carrying knives or other dangerous weapons. They dispatched these notices to all the captains of vessels entering the port and to the keepers of sailors' boarding houses. The Chairman of the Mercantile Marine Association vainly attempted to go further and requested legal power to inflict fines on those seen wearing, or carrying, sheath knives or dagger knives.

Such sailors, once in Liverpool, as seen above, presented many other serious problems. Particular concern was caused amongst those young constables who themselves were poorly educated and regularly fell to temptation or became unable to face the perils of their rigorous night duty. Few constables spoke the tongue of the visiting sailors and they were at a loss as to how they should handle those mariners such as the Spanish, who in June 1869, aroused complaints for playing pitch and toss in Cleveland Square.

Many sailors, themselves, in turn fell victims of the waterfront crimpers. With an average, in 1871, of 20,000 sailors ashore at almost any time, they developed a considerable reputation in the port for their manly qualities. Many of these deep-sea travellers, after being pent up on their ships for many months, came ashore laden with money to indulge in great excess. They readily met with the low prostitutes, some flaunting themselves in the doorways of their beer houses wearing only a petticoat and half-opened bedgown.

Boarding house keepers, often in league with infamous crimps, made the most of the gullible visitors. Both sides of many roads, such as Park Lane, became lined with well-known 'Cooking for Shipping' signs outside the keepers' houses. Others kept houses in Jamaica Street, Lower Parliament Street, Upper Frederick Street, Cleveland Square and the Anson Terrace districts. These keepers often sent out convicted thieves to deprive the official badge-wearing and licensed ships' porters of their daily work.

By way of protecting their livelihoods these porters helped the police with information. Working as either inwardboundmen, outboundmen, pierheadmen, or marketstuffmen, they came into contact with many sources of information as they attended the crews and passengers of numerous ships. Outwardbound porters attended those foreign vessels leaving the docks, the pierheads or lying in the river; the inwardbound porters attended the passengers arriving from foreign ports; the pierheads' porters assisted at the arrival of the coastal and river steamers; and the marketstuff porters awaited the offloading of fish and other market produce at the Landing Stage, at the Prince's Landing Stage and at the Clarence Dock.

Viciously opposed to them were the boarding house

Liverpool's Clarence Dock, c 1903
The Clarence Dock, opened in 1830, was another of the important docks to be designed by Jesse Hartley. It was the first on the historic waterfront to be entered from a half-tide basin. These basins, generally constructed for all the new docks built between 1830 and 1879, acted as both dock and lock. They were part of Hartley's attempt to reduce the number of dock river entrances and to increase the linkage between docks to speed up the turn-round time and reduce overcrowding. This splendid view shows the dock gates open and vessels floating on a high level of water.

keepers, their unlicensed porters and the crimps who
relentlessly pursued the most vulnerable of sailors as they
arrived from a long voyage. The unlicensed porters would
run to their paying boarding house master as soon as they
saw a newly-arrived long voyage vessel enter the Mersey.
Thereon they brought the master down to the ship. Once
the master had located new clients he rewarded his
informant with a portering job at the expense of the
official porters. The latter might then be further insulted
by being taunted as returned convicts or detectives for the
police. They were subjected to the latter taunt because,
after 1865, the official porters took the opportunity,
whenever it arose, to report the addresses of crimps to the
River Police. They did this particularly well in the cases of
those crimps difficult to trace, having apparently
disappeared, when a police summons had been taken out
against them. These badged porters also willingly
appeared in court with the river policemen to support
their information.

Inevitably, these porters had to face up to a series of
organised vengeful retaliations. They had to defend
themselves, for example, on those many occasions when a
vessel lay in an outside berth, some three or four ships
from the quayside. Without a river or dock policeman in
sight, gangs of 'loafers' gathered and launched fierce and
vicious sallies on the porters.

Any unsuspecting sailor, when not warned by the
licensed porters, or river police, might be taken at the first
opportunity by his boarding house master to an outfitters

for new clothes. Each master received a twenty percent commission on all purchases in these circumstances. If they failed to secure a newly-landed seaman as a boarder many masters went to prowl about and solicit in the Sailors' Home and earned a living in this manner. Such masters themselves became so vehemently opposed to the official porters, that when they had an outwardbound seaman heading for a vessel in Birkenhead Docks, they employed some of the worst characters on the pierheads rather than have the George's pierhead porters do their work.

In the last few hours of their stay in Liverpool the deep-sea sailors often became victims of the crimps. This was especially so before 1865. Until the riverpolice constables took on their duties, a foreign sailor being manhandled onto a vessel could summon little protection, particularly by night.

Liverpool became famous for crimping characters and those known as Shanghai Davies, Paddy Dreadnought, Dolan and MacNulty, became feared around Paradise Street as was Paddy Houlihan of Dennison Street. A certain John Da Costa, an American of Portuguese lineage, became infamous and was sung about by sailors in the famous shanty 'Heave Away Me Johnnies' for supplying crews for Yankee sailing ships.

Within a few years of the riverpolicemen commencing their duties, however, these brave constables had considerably helped to reduce the crimps' powers. By

1896, moreover, Head Constable John Nott-Bower, reported that they had entirely stamped out crimping.

Nevertheless, as the riverpolicemen succeeded in this duty, they in turn had their own staff numbers reduced. Initially, in the mid-sixties, two riverpolice crews went out on duty for eight hours, weather permitting, on each winter's day. In summer, they increased their shifts by one hour. The third crew rowed through the docks and on to the pierheads to supervise the opening of the dockgates and the masters in the berthing of their vessels.

When they had their own staff reduced, the riverpolicemen became less able to supervise the sailors and passengers on the river and at the pierheads. They also had less need to be involved with their original main duty, to prevent crimping, as the crews of the great sailing ships found themselves being superceded by those of the new ocean going and coastal steamers. Such steamship crews now found it more and more difficult to board their tallsided ships, usually tied up in the docks, unnoticed.

Head Constable John Nott-Bower, in 1895, suggested that the riverpolicemen should no longer work as a special body on the Mersey. By this time they could only visit a small number of those ships sailing in from deep waters and those they did they simply hailed, asked if all was correct and they moved on. In very foul weather, moreover, they could not get onto any vessels. Increasingly, too, they could not help the ships' captains from keeping off the unwanted traders who sought to board each ship as it berthed.

Despite the head constable recommending that his men should no longer serve as river policemen, they finally took charge of a much-needed steam launch, in 1899. Ironically, one crew of six policemen nearly drowned in January of the same year. Caught in a gale in the afternoon of January the 2nd, on the river near Tranmere, they had to run south and shelter alongside a flatboat named Margaret. They found themselves trapped there and throughout the afternoon and night they had to bail to keep afloat. A boat set out to look for the missing men in the evening but, in the dark, the crew could not find them. Eventually, suffering from cold and exposure and helped by the crew of the Margaret, they returned to the Liverpool Landing Stage at 7a.m. on January the 3rd.

In time the river policemen, like the Albert Dock they helped to protect, became more and more overshadowed by the growing use of steamships and the decline of the sailing vessels. Ironically, it was when the police acquired their steam launch that they began to witness the very end of the great days of fully rigged sailing ships on the River Mersey.

10

An improved Liverpool Waterfront

To safeguard Prince Albert from any source of physical
danger during his visit to Liverpool, in 1846, the Prince's
special committee wrote to the Liverpool Watch
Committee asking that secure policing arrangements be
made. So successfully did Head Constable Maurice
Dowling undertake these arrangements that immediately
after the Prince's visit the watch committee recorded their
appreciation of his 'zealous and indefatigable exertions'.
This was a considerable achievement in view of
Liverpool's notoriety for public disorder at this time.

Liverpool, of course, was by no means unique in the
United Kingdom in the threats it faced to public order and
the number of outrages committed against life and
property. At this time in Britain many criminals still
operated, in unpoliced areas. Deepsea sailors and
travellers attempting to reach the Liverpool waterfront
faced many serious threats even before they had entered
the River Mersey estuary.

Ship wreckers and looters on the North Wales coasts and
those of Lancashire and Cheshire, constantly plundered
vessels as they ran aground in a region of many coastal
sandbanks. In these days of great international maritime

Canning Dock and The Port of Liverpool Building, c 1909
The sailing ship Sorlandet majestically dominates the foreground of this corner of
the Canning Dock. Sailing vessels regularly underwent repairs in the two Canning
Graving Docks leading from it. The Canning Dock itself was relatively small in size
and the space inside was further reduced by the need to keep two of its passages
clear. The dock was also used for importing building materials and by fishing
vessels, schooners and dredgers.

The Canning Half-Tide Dock and Custom House
This museum photograph depicts the use made by sailing ships of the Canning
Half-Tide Dock, c 1880. The Georgian building dominating the background is the
Old Custom House constructed on the site of Liverpool's first dock. During World
War II it was badly damaged and later demolished. The Half-Tide Dock is today
overlooked by the world-famous Merseyside Maritime Museum.

travel Liverpool policemen had to act regularly upon instructions to hire carriages and take boats to determine whether a Liverpool-bound vessel was in distress or not.

When any disaster did occur it was not unknown for as many as 300 to 400 coastal inhabitants to take part in the looting of ship's cargoes consisting of casks of wine and rum, cotton bales, tobacco casks and goods of almost every description. These local villagers added to the anxiety of the travellers by also indulging in terrifying acts of savagery. When the Grecian was wrecked on the Cheshire coast in the thirties, the ship's master, Captain Salisbury, was drowned. Whilst his body lay on the shore awaiting transport to an inquest, it was stripped, a finger was cut off and a ring was stolen.

In November, 1856, on the same coast, five Liverpool policemen journeyed to the shipwrecked vessels Silas Wright and S. M. Fox. They boarded these vessels, aground on the Great Burbo sandbank, to prevent looters from stealing the ships' cargoes. The port of Liverpool's underwriters became especially anxious to safeguard the cargo on the Silas since they valued it at £100,000. Other looters included those in Liverpool who pretended to be fishermen but kept 'speculative boats' and sold any plunder they gathered to those known receivers who kept marine stores.

By the end of the century, fortunately, the general quality of life on Liverpool's waterfront had improved. No longer, for example, as in the late thirties and early forties, did hundreds of convicted prisoners have to face transportation for such crimes as brothel keeping, theft or counterfeiting of coin. Such unfortunates, who had included boys as young as thirteen years of age, had usually been placed in irons, in Kirkdale Gaol, upon conviction. Later, as they awaited a ship to take them to the colonies, they had their irons removed but wore instead a small shackle, or ring, riveted just above one of their ankles as their badge of conviction.

Any truculent gaol prisoner, moreover, might additionally be punished by the turnkeys there. These men used a whip-like, many-tongued scourge on the adult offenders, or the birch on the young ones. Other gaol prisoners, too, might face capital punishment there. On such occasions the turnkeys would thrust several ponderous black beams through the gaol's outer wall to await the hangman's ropes. Those executed would finally be buried, without memorial, within the southwestern angle of the gaol's walls.

Fortunately, the quality of life for many dockside children steadily improved. Though thousands of barefooted and raggedly dressed children still begged in the streets of the seaport in the nineties, fewer children had to sleep without shelter. No longer did Liverpool's citizens then have to witness gangs of 'street arabs' or vagabond children, such as those seen by night in the mid-fifties thronging Canning Place, outside the Sailors' Home.

In these circumstances as opportunity afforded, typical

youngsters there had to earn a few pence by carrying goods, holding horses' reins, or selling matches. Whenever possible, they paid twopence to sleep in one of the nearby lodging houses. When penniless they had to sleep in the open. If the weather was suitable they slept on the warm flagstones outside the bakery on the corner of Canning Place. When the weather was wet they might enter a yard near the Sailors' Home and use empty barrels there as shelters.

Those sailors who stayed in the Home, of course, often fell prey themselves to either those former convicts acting as unofficial ships' porters, to the unscrupulous boarding house keepers, to the sailors' girls or to the crimps who infested these dockland districts. Fortunately, by the end of the century, according to Head Constable John Nott-Bower, crimes of violence committed in Liverpool had noticeably fallen since the eighties.

Nott-Bower also reported that the sailors' girls had become less notorious on Liverpool's riverfront. Much of the latter improvement was achieved by the fundamental work of the charitable ladies in Liverpool, such as the remarkable Josephine Butler and her associates. In the early sixties she had begun her successful campaign for moral purity in the oakum sheds of the Liverpool Workhouse. Mrs. Butler and her supporters had become particularly anxious to succeed in their campaign when they discovered that many children, sometimes as young as three years of age, had fallen under the control of the brothel keepers.

During the latter part of Queen Victoria's reign it became
noticeable, too, that the activities of Liverpool's dockland
fireraisers had been significantly curtailed. Liverpool
firepolicemen, police warehouse patrols and even the
river police had helped to reduce the careless use of fires
at the docks. Liverpool's dock policemen, for example,
even became responsible for searching porters,
warehousemen and dockers for pipes and matches. In
1866, two especially appointed dock policemen found
more than 120 pipes and a similar quantity of 'lucifer'
matches being illegally carried by workers into the
Liverpool warehouses.

At the same time the small body of Liverpool detective
constables, often operating in disguise at the docks,
successfully pursued those who undertook warehouse
robberies on a somewhat grand scale. In the winter
months of 1867, for example, they helped to trace and
recover £2,000 worth of cotton that had been stolen and
taken to Birmingham, Sheffield and some other large
towns.

In addition, they successfully dealt with those gangs
which had stolen large quantities of grain from
Liverpool's docks and they arrested the members of
another gang which had systematically scuttled ships.
Other Liverpool detectives pursued many of those
fugitives from different parts of the United Kingdom who
sought to escape overseas. In 1866, in total, the detectives
assisted in some 303 such cases and some of their

colleagues sailed as far as New York, Montreal and Jamaica to continue their 'enquiries'.

This improving professionalism of the police force greatly discouraged wrongdoers and proved a contributory factor, together with various social and economic improvements, in reducing known crimes in Victorian Liverpool. However, there were still dockland streets in the port even in the 1890's which were unsafe for respectable persons to enter and which the police could not patrol alone. Nevertheless, by the end of the century Liverpool's public places such as those at or near St. George's Hall, Lime Street, Williamson Square, and the Custom House (close to the Albert Dock), generally became safer for visitors, seafarers and citizens alike to visit at will.

The Pierhead Liverpool, c 1915
This fine view of Liverpool's waterfront captures the Pierhead as a flourishing centre of commercial activity. The River Mersey, in the background, is filled with a variety of vessels. At the Prince's Landing Stage a large passenger steamship is berthed north of the ferryboat. The dependence of the river vessels on steam is now most apparent.

11

Prosperity returns to the Albert Dock

The Albert Dock's prosperity from the handling and storage of off-loaded cargoes was inextricably linked – as Nancy Richie-Noakes has so expertly explained – to the popularity, with traders, of the deepsea sailing ships of between 500 and 1000-ton cargo capacity. By the 1890's more than sixty per cent of the vessels using Liverpool still harnessed sail but this percentage dramatically declined in the last two decades of the nineteenth century. When Liverpool entered the twentieth century, less than ten per cent of the port's shipping was dependent upon sail power.

Such 'old fashioned' ships could no longer match the greater efficiency of the ocean-going steam ships. The latter were cheaper to run and were better fitted to make use of the growing number of quayside transit sheds. These sheds, too, were more easily served by dockers using the improved cargo-handling equipment. Then, as the northern docks expanded to cater for the larger steamships, the twentieth century increasingly witnessed the demise of the Albert Dock.

Some unusual successes continued to occur at the Dock. Firstly, in 1897, in keeping with the Albert Dock

Albert Dock, Liverpool, c 1908
This photograph shows the north-east stack of the Albert warehouse, after conversion in 1899, by the Riverside Cold Storage and Ice Co. Parts of this building were lined with timber and cork for insulation. On the top floor the refrigeration and ice-making machinery were then installed and the ice manufactured there was moved through an electric-operating machine and down to the ships' holds by way of a chute.

Sailing vessels outside Block D of the Albert warehouses overlooking the Maritime Park, 1991.

fire-fighting traditions, innovatory fire-engine experiments were undertaken there. At the suggestion of the deputy superintendent of the Liverpool Fire Brigade, Chief Inspector Thomas, the steam-engine 'Hornby' was supplied with water direct from the Albert Dock's mains pipes. This supply, rather than the traditional 'dams' of water in the docks themselves, shortened the time for getting the engine to pump out water through the hose-pipes. There was also little wasted water, or 'overflow', and the fire hoses could be supplied with the pressurised mains water even if the engine had to be stopped. This improved method of 'feeding' the fire-engine earned Inspector Thomas the magnificent reward of five pounds for this, his revolutionary idea!

In the following year, in 1898, the Riverside Cold Storage and Ice Co., made use of the Albert Dock northeast stacks' top floor. There it housed its refrigeration and ice-making machinery. Users of the cold-store came to include the Liverpool Steam Fishing Company, the importers of Irish bacon and butter and some shippers of meat carcasses from the River Plate, South America.

After 1920 the Albert Dock was used by only a few ships on a commercial basis. Those vessels that did berth either awaited a graving dock placement or were on Mersey Docks and Harbour Board duty. Additional 'dangerous years' did recur for the Albert Dock in the form of Enemy air-raids on Liverpool during the Second World War and some damage was incurred by two warehouse blocks. Hundreds of low-tonnage Admiralty ships – including merchant ships, landing craft and small warships – used the Dock during the hostilities. Fortunately, the Dock complex survived the bombing raids, especially the Blitz of May 1941 though other nearby City buildings such as the Custom House in Canning Place, were destroyed. After the war the Dock could fulfil few of the modern docking requirements and it eventually closed in 1972.

Thanks to the partnership of the Arrowcroft Group and the Merseyside Development Corporation, the Albert Dock was superbly refurbished in the 1980's and has come to stand at the centre of the re-development of the Merseyside docks. Once again, as in 1846, when the Prince Consort opened the Dock, it became a focus of interest worthy of visits from several members of The Royal Family. Inevitably, local senior police officers became responsible for coordinating the royal visitors' security arrangements.

A series of sparkling events followed rapidly. The Tall Ships arrived in the River Mersey on 1 August 1984, for four days of joint activities between the European and Atlantic fleets. Her Majesty, The Queen and His Royal Highness, the Duke of Edinburgh visited Merseyside for the opening of the International Garden Festival, the Queen Elizabeth II Law Courts and to review the Tall Ships' Parade in the River Mersey. Whilst many thousands of people viewed the ships in the Vittoria and Albert Docks, the march of their crews from the Pier Head to the Philharmonic Hall – for a prize-giving ceremony – was watched by so many members of the public that the City centre came to a halt.

Liverpool's Canning Half-Tide Dock, 1984
The internationally famous Merseyside Maritime Museum, housed in the Albert
Dock North Warehouse is pictured in the background to this scene. This official
Museum photograph depicts the continued link with Liverpool's sailing ship
history. The vessels were some of those to visit the seaport during the 1984 Tall
Ships' Race.

The Albert Dock looking northwest towards the Port of Liverpool and Liver Buildings.

Police officers estimated that over half a million spectators flocked to the banks of the River Mersey to witness this spectacular event. Enhancing the culmination of the event was Her Majesty the Queen's presence aboard the Royal Yacht Britannia, reviewing the Tall Ships' departure from the River Mersey.

Two years later, in 1986, the superbly refurbished Albert Dock was awarded the prestigious European Gold Medal for the Restoration of Historic Monuments by the F V S Foundation, Hamburg. As a multi-million pound development it attracted some two million visitors in the same year. The visitors' interest no doubt centred not only in marvelling at the scale of the dock buildings – the largest Grade One listed buildings in the United Kingdom – but the ingenious transformation that had occurred throughout the Dock.

On 24 May 1988, His Royal Highness the Prince of Wales visited the complex to re-open the Dock. Prince Charles then opened the Tate Gallery, housed in the west warehouse stack and he visited a Prince's Trust National Trade Exhibition. His Royal Highness – as Prince Albert before him – dined at the Dock, taking lunch at the Wharf Restaurant. In November 1989 Her Royal Highness Princess Margaret came to open the Art and the Sea Gallery in the Maritime Museum.

The security of all such royal visits relied upon expert police planning. The 1846 visit was the responsibility of Maurice Dowling, Liverpool's Chief Constable. The 1980's visits owed much to Kenneth Oxford, Chief Constable of Merseyside, and his senior police officers.

Fortunately, for present day visitors the dangers of the Victorian era have disappeared from the locality. Nearby place names are often the only reminders of the drinking dens, the gambling resorts, the sailors' lodging houses and the houses of ill-repute that menaced the visitors in the sailing ship era. The 'traps' set every night for unsuspecting sailors, as described by Charles Dickens in 'The Uncommercial Traveller' have long since disappeared.

By contrast, todays' visitors have the opportunity to shop for fashions and furnishings, for works of art and antiques, and to eat well in a comfort and style undreamt-of by the many who made use of the Albert Dock in the Victorian era.

Inside the complex, contemporary visitors may find a host of interesting settings in which to meet their friends. These features include The Dock Traffic Office, added in 1848 and which is now the home of Granada Television's News Centre, and the Cooperage and Dock Master's House added in 1852. For somewhere new to eat, to treat children to 'burgers' or pizzas, to hold a business lunch, wedding reception or candle-lit supper –   the Albert Dock is able to offer a wide choice of interesting places. These include an atmospheric wine-bar in an authentic cellar; pubs; an International Food Court featuring

Chinese, Italian and American Style dishes plus pancakes, patisserie and soft drinks bar.

As for the shops, an immense range of goods which includes diamond rings – speciality teas – French perfumes – cameras – Australian crystal – original oil paintings – nautical instruments – Japanese Kimonos – cuddly toys – posters and cards – heraldic shields – embroidered linen – antique prints – fruit and flowers – sweets and chocolate – are just part of the present-day dazzling display in the myriad of shops and brightly-coloured coster carts. The historic and commercial splendours of the Albert Dock are thus now to be admired from the ease and comfort of the most tasteful of modern fittings.

The successful developments within the Albert Dock continue to increase. **Anything to Declare? is a prime example.** This new National Museum of H.M. Customs and Excise opened in 1993 within the Albert Dock's D Block. Phase One covers the work of contemporary customs officers. Both phases appear set to maintain the spectacular progress achieved at the Albert Dock.

12

The Return of the Tall Ships

The historic Albert Dock complex became a particular favourite with sightseers when the Tall Ships visited the River Mersey in 1984 and 1992. Many visitors travelled hundreds of miles to take part in these unique events. Until 1984 such a gathering of so many beautiful vessels, with their towering masts and billowing sails had not been seen on the river for more than eighty years.

On the first of these special occasions some 25 tall, deep draught ships sailed into the river estuary. They had journeyed from Nova Scotia, in Canada, to complete the final leg of what was known as The Cutty Sark Tall Ships' Race. These vessels immediately awakened a deep-rooted sense of nostalgia with those spectators who flocked to see them moored from 1st.-4th. August, 1984 at the Vittoria Dock in Birkenhead.

Nearly 40 other smaller ships had joined them after they had travelled from Greenock, in Scotland, in the finale of their own European race. This joint venture was the first in modern times in which two such sail-training fleets had converged on a major British port. The newly restored Albert Dock, with its adjacent Canning Dock became home to many of the smaller vessels. These historic docks were thus filled to capacity for the first time since their prime in the nineteenth century.

Both the large and small sailing craft proved themselves to be outstanding attractions. In just one day, a staggering 60,000 visitors travelled to board those sailing vessels moored on both sides of the River Mersey. This celebration was one of a series of events in 1984 that was deeply nostalgic for both the Birkenhead and Liverpool communities. Liverpool A.F.C. had won the Football League Championship, Everton A.F.C. had won the F.A. Cup and the Liverpool based International Garden Festival was in full bloom when the Tall Ships arrived.

For many persons, these ships awakened a sense of identity with the region's maritime heritage. The calendar of special events also helped to reinforce their mounting interest. Vast crowds thronged the Pierhead, for example, to watch the ships' crews begin their combined march through the city. The final event, The Majestic Parade of Sail, drew dense crowds to line both banks of the river to salute those courageous young crews and seafarers in particular who had helped navigate their vessels through the three thousand miles of heaving swells and sudden terrifying squalls that relentlessly occur in one of the world's most cruel seas – the North Atlantic Ocean.

Watching the spectacular finale – when the 63-strong combined fleets staged their Grand Parade of Sail – led by the Sail-Training Association's Winston Churchill – was H.R.H. The Queen aboard the Royal Yacht Britannia in the Mersey. Her presence symbolised – as Prince Albert had in 1846 when he entered the Albert Dock aboard the Royal Yacht, Fairy – the magnificent seafaring traditions of the British Royal Family. One of the most poignant moments resulted as hundreds of thousands of spectators joined to sing the famous local sea ballad, The Leaving of Liverpool.

The sheer numbers of land-based crowds led to eventual traffic chaos on an unprecendented scale. Wallasey came to a standstill as roads were choked with vehicles and cars tailed back for several miles on the M53. With emergency vehicles trapped, a pregnant woman who went into labour had to be taken to a train at New Brighton to help her to hospital.

River ferryboat services, a principal means of transporting spectators across the Mersey, ran well beyond normal hours in a bid to help people home after the evening's firework display. Many of those who believed that their memories might be a once-in-a-lifetime experience were grateful to find this was not necessarily so. Fortunately, the plans to stage a second international sailing ship race had already been put forward in 1982. This race was to be widely regarded by many as a fitting occasion to mark the 500th anniversary of Christopher Columbus' historic voyage to the Americas in 1492. Columbus was regarded by many as the famous fifteenth century admiral who transformed the map of the world by discovering the Americas. Others however, regarded him as a ruthless profiteer who wiped out native Indians in whatever lands he reached.

The Tall Ships of course belonged to a later era. Two people in particular were recognized as being responsible for organizing their return to the twin communities of Birkenhead and Liverpool, in 1992. Firstly, Portuguese entrepreneur, Dr. Luis Lobarto put forward the idea of staging the finale of the international maritime celebration on Merseyside. Nigel Green, as will be seen below, organised the calendar of special events on Merseyside.

Sea-loving Dr. Lobarto, a professor of civil engineering who had been elected President of the Portuguese Sail Training Association, had proposed that Liverpool should be the major destination for the ships' return to Europe "because it was historically connected with the mass European migration of the 18th. and 19th. centuries to colonise America". In both these centuries Liverpool's links with the U.S.A. had from time to time been surrounded by controversy. When trade and the conveyance of immigrants to the United States rapidly developed in the second half of the 18th. and early 19th. centuries, the reputation of the port became marred by those British shipowners who indulged in the ignominious African Trade. This involved the carrying of negro slaves from West Africa to both the Indies and Southern States of North America. By the latter half of the 18th. century Liverpool's traffic had increased to such proportions that it was unchallenged as the leading exponent of the trade.

Such deplorable activities were openly condemned by many of the port's leading citizens and a number fought hard for its abolition. Perhaps no-one was more conscientious than William Roscoe, one of Liverpool's most distinguished persons. With William Rathbone II and III – father and son – they founded in 1787 the Society for the Abolition of the Slave Trade. One year later William Wilberforce led his own campaign, supported by Roscoe, to help secure the eventual outlawing of the trade in Britain in 1807.

Meanwhile the numbers of those European passengers bound for the U.S.A. from Liverpool continued to increase. This was particularly so, after 1825, when the anti-emigration laws were relaxed by the British Government. Soon many of Liverpool's shipping companies were competing for custom. The emigration movement reached its peak in the 1840's and 1850's. Though many emigrants originated from England, Scotland, Wales and Ireland, other Europeans – Germans, Scandinavians, Poles, Hungarians, Czechs, Romanians, Austrians, Greeks and Italians swelled the numbers of those in temporary residence in the Liverpool Dockside Wards. It was in this period that Liverpool's municipal conscience stirred as a series of disasters – such as those in fire-ravaged warehouses – further sullied Liverpool's reputation. Between 1819 and 1859, when an estimated five million emigrants sailed to the United States and nearly half-a- million to Canada – some two-thirds of these journeyed from Liverpool. The majority of these sailed "steerage class" and their accommodation was usually very crude on the sailing ships of the era. Up to one thousand might be crowded below decks on any one ship.

Liverpool's diplomatic relations with the United States were sorely tested during the bloody years of the American Civil War, 1861-65. Whilst Britain remained officially neutral the rebellious Southern States, the Confederacy, openly encouraged support from the British merchants. A number of those using the seaport's facilities had close ties with the American South because of the British textile industry's dependence on southern, slave-grown cotton.

In the first half of the 19th century the manufacture of cotton textiles was the most important single item of British foreign trade. From 1820 to 1850 Liverpool had handled at least 80 per cent of the U.K's raw cotton imports. Thus for many years the import of this cargo remained a primary source of Liverpool's prosperity.

When President Lincoln proclaimed a blockade of the Confederacy's southern coast it eventually cut the import of raw cotton into Liverpool by half. The seaport became a hot-bed of intrigue as the Confederate establishment in Liverpool undertook to encourage British firms to 'blockade run'. Southern agents placed advertisements in local newspapers offering advice and assistance to companies willing to take part in this clandestine trade.

Captain James Bullock of the Confederate Navy arrived in

Liverpool, 3rd. June 1861, with orders to obtain warships for use against Northern shipping. Within a month he had placed an order for the construction of the steamer Oreto at William C. Miller and Company's shipyard. This ship was to become the successful commerce raider, re-named the Florida. Later the Alabama was built in the yard of Birkenhead's John Laird. Thereafter followed the British-built iron-clad warships the 'Laird rams'. In 1873 a Geneva tribunal awarded the U.S.A. a total of 15 million dollars for depredations committed by the warships Alabama, Florida and Shenandoah. These had been allowed to arm and then escape from British ports.

After this war, Liverpool managed to regain its position as the main port for transatlantic trade with the U.S.A. and this in time saw further tens of thousands of emigrants flock into the port. They came seeking passage to a new life in a new land, many of them fleeing from poverty, oppression and religious persecution. In total in the hundred years until 1930 no less then nine million emigrants sailed out from the River Mersey, mostly to either America, Canada, Australia, New Zealand or South Africa. It was this historical connection with Liverpool that convinced Dr. Lobarto that Liverpool should be chosen as the European destination of the Columbus Regatta, 1992.

Merseyside's Nigel Green, having successfully organized the 1984 Tall Ships' Visit, seemed the perfect choice to manage the second visit in 1992. An enthusiastic ambassador for the region he had forseen the occasion as one that could dramatically boost the economy of the area. He was also the inspiration behind the annual Mersey River Festival, entering its 12th year by 1992. It was fitting that as chairman of the Mersey Executive Committee he and his team were to oversee every aspect of the 1992 five-day event in the Columbus Regatta's last port of call.

He and the members of his committee rightly regarded the return of the Tall Ships to the Mersey as a spectacle which would again sell the region on an international scale and encourage vital investment. This was the message also promoted by the Merseyside Development Corporation. Bob Lane, M.D.C. head of external affairs, also made every effort to ensure the calendar of special events ran smoothly. He felt co-operation was the keyword. M.D.C. and its co-promoters, the Borough of Wirral, Mersey Docks and Harbour Company and Liverpool City Council worked with the local emergency services, the public transport operators and the Mersey Tourism Board to achieve a spectacular and trouble-free event.

The eyes of the world were thus again to be focused firmly on the Tall Ships' return to Merseyside, August 12th to 16th 1992. A 'feast of fun' was fittingly planned to coincide with their presence in the Mersey. On August 12th, the first day of the calendar a charity concert to celebrate the silver jubilee of the BBC's local station, Radio Merseyside, was hosted by the Merseyside Youth Orchestra and held at the King's Dock. At Birkenhead's

Vittoria Dock official welcoming receptions, followed by a barbeque, were held for the ships' crews. On the following day a civic reception for the ships' captains was held at Wallasey Town Hall. In the afternoon the Littlewoods' Offshore Trophy – the Liverpool to the Isle of Man Yacht Race – began at the Coburg Dock. In the evening a Royal Navy ball was held at St. George's Hall, Liverpool.

On Friday 14th August, a one-day conference, entitled Liverpool – The Maritime City, was hosted at the Mersey Maritime Museum within the Albert Dock. A feast of music, Fanfare for a New World, a gala performance hosted by Sir Peter Ustinov featured a host of world famous singers at the King's Dock. Heading the celebrities in the operatic spectacular were Montserrat Caballe, Rita Hunter, Dennis O'Neil and Paco Pena. The stage for their performance was built to resemble a great ship and featured especially constructed screens on which great projections paid tribute to the music of America, Spain and Great Britain. Sir Charles Mackerras and Julian Reynolds conducted the concert extravaganza.

The following day, Saturday 15th August, more than 1,000 crew members, accompanied by the Band of the Royal Marines assembled at Chavasse Gardens in Liverpool before their parade through the city centre. At midday they arrived at St. George's Hall for the Columbus Regatta Awards Ceremony. An ecumenical Service of Thanksgiving was held at the Metropolitan Cathedral in the early evening and later there was an Ocean Fantasia

– Music for the Tall Ships – a premiere concert by the
Liverpool Royal Philharmonic Orchestra held at the
Philharmonic Hall. At Wallasey there was a Tall Ships'
Ball at the Town Hall. At 10pm on the River Mersey there
was a fireworks display, set to music and simultaneously
staged from three separate points; New Brighton's Fort
Perch Rock, the mid river between the Liverpool Pierhead
and Wallasey's Town Hall and south of the Albert Dock
and the King's Dock.

Late on Saturday the Tall Ships began to take their
positions in the river in preparation for the Grand Parade
of Sail on Sunday. A salute to their presence was given by
the fleet air display over the River Mersey at midday 16th
August. This included a prestigious assembly of Royal
Navy and Royal Air Force craft.

The most spectacular event of the visit – The Grand
Parade of Sail – was organized to take place between
2pm. and 5pm. The Parade was to be augmented by both
civilian and Royal Navy sailing vessels. It was only fitting
that King Juan Carlos and Queen Sophia of Spain – the
King was the patron of Grand Regatta Columbus 1992 and
had come to Liverpool to join the celebrations – were
aboard their Royal Yacht moored at the Pierhead and
witnessed the Salute to the Grand Parade.

Among the combined fleets was the largest Tall Ship in
the world, the Sedov from the CIS. Nearly 20 more such
class A vessels from throughout Europe, South America
and the Middle East joined with the ship.

The leading British ship in the Regatta was the Greater Manchester Challenge, sponsored by the Liverpool-based food firm John West. Together with its sister ship, The Francis Drake, they had comfortably navigated the hazardous waters of their 10,000 mile round trip. Their voyage had taken them via Lisbon, Cadiz and the Canary Islands before crossing the Atlantic to Puerto Rico. Then it was on to New York and Boston before the final leg home. These were the only two vessels to have started and finished in Liverpool – from their base at the Bramley Moore Dock.

Their return and the sight of the other large majestic ships on the River Mersey had thus provided an insight, a glimpse back in time, to the heyday of Sail. These visiting vessels had helped to supply the catalyst that awakened in many sightseers a deeper appreciation of the local maritime heritage that enriches the Liverpool and Wirral waterfronts.

Remarkably, plans were soon afloat to stage a similar Tall Ships Race to mark the start of the new millenium in the year 2000. With a regular eight year interval beginning to occur between such races the organizers now dubbed these events as The Water Olympics. Plans were also being promoted to create a permanent berth to welcome individual Tall Ships on a frequent basis. In Wirral it was felt that the world's largest sailing vessels should come to regard Merseyside as their trans-oceanic destination after each of their long voyages. When Poland's Mlodzienzy tied up for three days at Birkenhead's West Float in Easter

1993 she attracted large bank holiday crowds. This was prior to her setting sail for Las Palmas, Bermuda and the U.S.A.

The attractiveness of such vessels in the regenerated historic docks along the River Mersey's Waterfront had proved to be increasingly popular with sightseers. They had also helped to promote a deeper understanding of the development of sailing ships both in the United Kingdom and in other parts of the world. The South Docks of Liverpool – with the Albert Dock precinct at their heart – served to create a unique and authentic setting for the smaller sailing vessels. With their own restored 'resident' ships, original technological fittings and artefacts the South Docks have become a valuable time capsule for admirers to appreciate the endeavours and genius that were essential to create an internationally famous seaport. Liverpool, once known as The Port of the Thousand Ships, again began to enjoy increasing numbers of international admirers. Some of these, with the Tall Ships of 1984 and 1992, may be seen in Chapter 13.

13

The Albert Dock's World Famous Attractions

Any visit to the Albert Dock should be an exciting experience. With so much to see it may be difficult to know where to start. A short walk inside the Britannia Pavilion will take the visitor to the Tourist Information Centre. Here the variety of opportunities for shopping and the facilities for eating will be explained. There are four world-famous attractions: in alphabetical order these are, Animation World, the Beatle's Story, the Merseyside Maritime Museum and Tate Gallery Liverpool.

Animation World:
The outer central cart bay at the Britannia Pavilion allows access to two of the Albert Dock's most famous attractions. To the right of the courtyard is Animation World. Visitors may here approach this "definitely different" feature by descending steps to the basement or vaults. Young and old alike have the rare opportunity to enjoy a fascinating trip into the colourful world of animation. This is where they have the chance to meet Danger Mouse, the Big Friendly Giant, Duckula and Toad of Toad Hall. Here there are "hands-on" exhibits, studio displays and a shop which helps to create a unique insight into the art of the animator. This is a "must" for all those young-at-heart visitors.

The Beatles' Story:
For those who are avid fans of The Fab Four, and those who are curious to find out what the "fuss" was about, the Story is a remarkable glimpse into the past. This is a walk-through experience which helps to create the sights, sounds and the smells of the swinging 60s.

Here is the chance to experience one of the most sensational stories that the world of popular music has ever known. The exhibition has a replica of the original Cavern Club in Liverpool's Matthew Street where the tale began. Visitors can re-live The Beatles' meteoric rise to fame with a nostalgic journey along their route to success. This includes a trip to Hamburg, in Germany, the growth of Beatlemania and the groups "tune in" to the flower power cult of their later years. The Beatles' Story is regarded as Liverpool's lasting tribute to the City's most famous "pop-music" sons – John Lennon, Paul McCartney, George Harrison and Ringo Starr.

It is also a unique venue in which company or private parties may meet. In the replica of the original Cavern Club such occasions will allow party-goers to match the festive mood of the "swinging 60s".

The Beatles' Story is an "undercover" all-year attraction in the Britannia Vaults, from 10.00am to 6.00pm. There is also a souvenir shop and access facilities for the disabled.

The Merseyside Maritime Museum:
This has grown in a short period of time to become world

famous. It is respected for its dedication to the history of the great Port of Liverpool, its ships and its people.

The museum has developed a unique blend of archives, video displays, historic quaysides and collections of nautical artifacts. What follows is a brief description of its historical evolvement and its present day attractions.

A Maritime Museum for Liverpool had first been suggested in the late nineteenth century. Little progress was made with this idea until 1913 when the City Centre Museum established a shipping gallery. By the end of the 1930s the need for a separate Maritime Museum had become paramount.

The Second World War, 1939-45, and the heavy enemy aircraft bombing raids on Liverpool delayed any further progress. The William Brown Street City Centre Museum suffered serious damage and a substantial part of the shipping models' collection was destroyed. It was several decades later before a waterfront site was acquired and renovated to form part of today's Merseyside Maritime Museum.

The efforts of the Merseyside County Council under the leadership of Sir Kenneth Thompson led to the opening of the first phase of the Maritime Museum in July 1980. This phase incorporated the renovation of the Pilotage Building, the Boat Shed and those quayside and dock areas to the immediate north of the Canning Dock Half-Tide Basin.

At this point in time the Merseyside County Council recognised that Block D, or the north warehouse stack of the Albert Dock should become the main building for the Record Office and the principal galleries of the Maritime Museum.

After a start was made in 1982 this building was restored in two stages by the twin agencies of the M.D.C. and the Merseyside Task Force. The M.D.C. became responsible for the installation of services, including gas, water and electricity, and for the galleries.

Both processess involved major changes to facilitate the comfortable use of the building by several hundreds of thousands of visitors each year. This was far removed from the original use of the site by several hundred dock workers, sailors, carters and the like in the Victorian era.

The main warehouse structures were surveyed and found to rest soundly – surrounded by the clay and timber piles they were built on in the 1840's. Yet there were still some major problems to overcome before they could be used as a modern tourist attraction. The Maritime Museum block was the only warehouse, however, to retain its original roof. This was not before the tiny lattice girders to which it had been riveted when first under construction had been restored. The brick vault of each ceiling, found to have wrought iron tie-rods above and below had been so strongly attached that the exterior brickwork was able to be grit-blasted for its present day

The Albert Dock Liverpool

Stone walled Dock Gateman's hut

Quayside Capstan

The Edmund Gardner No2 Pilot Boat

A Pitcher boiler

Some interesting aspects of the Dock area.

page 128

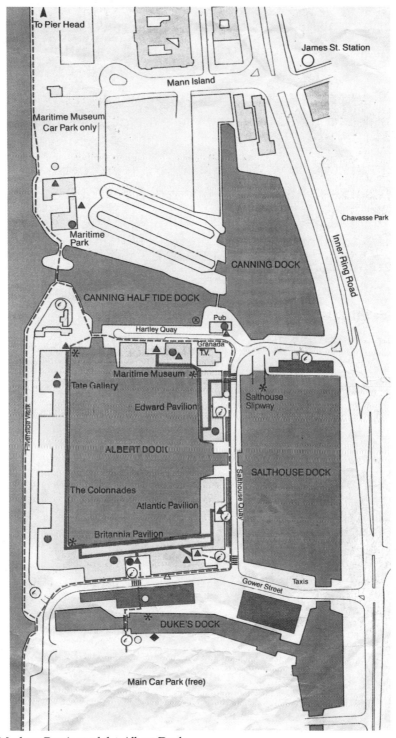

The Modern Precinct of the Albert Dock

beautiful finished effect. There was no need either for the repointing of the brickwork after this grit-blasting process.

The visitor may welcome a brief outline of the principal galleries in the Museum and these are described below:

Emigrants to a New World: In 1986 the first permanent gallery of the Museum was opened in part of the basement of Block D. Entitled Emigrants to a New World, this award-winning gallery portrays the story of emigration through the Port of Liverpool, 1830-1930, by nine million emigrants. There are three main parts to enjoy. Firstly, there is a survey of the emigrants themselves, their places of origin, the lure that drew them from poverty and persecution in Europe to their passage through Liverpool. The reconstruction of their experiences in Liverpool is shown. There is a chance for visitors to re-live the past in a walk through the reconstructed, narrow, dimly lit lodginghouse streets, the quaysides and then across a catwalk bridge onto the emigrant U.S.A.-bound sailing ship, the Shackamaxon of Philadelphia.

On board in the cramped bowels of the wooden ship, visitors may find themselves face to face with live emigrants in the shape of role- playing characters. The bright hopes and gnawing fears which accompanied the terror of weeks at sea for many who might never have seen a ship or sea, let alone set sail to cross an ocean, are re-lived.

At the end of their voyage, the surviving emigrants usually faced the trials of confronting Immigration Officials to secure their status as new emigrants.

Other exhibitions include: 'Liverpool 1207-1857, the Evolution of the Port'; Liverpool's importance is traced from its early history as a fishing village. At the time of King John, in 1207, Letters Patent were issued by him to mark the growing status of the town. The end of the period, in 1857, recognised the end of an era in Liverpool's growth because in the following year the Mersey Docks and Harbour Board was created. This stemmed from the widespread concern that the Liverpool Dock Trustees had, by this time, become unrepresentative of the widening range of docks users. Thereafter one single authority, the Mersey Docks and Harbour Board, became responsible for the docks on both sides of the River Mersey.

The World of Models: This rare collection displays some 200 of those ships models from the previous extensive collection that suffered damage in the aerial bombing raids of the Second World War, 1939-45. The original display in the Liverpool City Centre Museum had, in the 1930s, received international acclaim. The models, including one of the ill-fated ship the Titanic, are anchored in glass cases.

The Builders of Great Ships Gallery reveals how ship building on the River Mersey progressed from the time of

Canning Basin and Custom house, c 1890
This scene shows several contrasts. Inside the basin, humble 'flat' vessels occupy the places once filled by ocean-going merchant ships. The magnificent Georgian Custom House overlooks the tall brick-built chimney of the Pumphouse on the right. Constructed in 1878, the latter was designed to provide the waterpower for the new hydraulic hoists and pulleys used for handling the Albert Dock cargoes.

Salthouse Dock and Custom house, c 1900
The Salthouse Dock, as this picture suggests, was constricted by its limited size throughout its history. It received its name from the role it played in the growth of the Liverpool salt trade. With the completion of the adjacent Albert Dock in 1846, it became the loading centre for those ocean-going sailing ships which had offloaded their imports into the new dock. When this photograph was taken Salthouse had probably reverted to being used by coastal and Irish trading ships.

Salthouse Dock, c 1907
This is the view, looking south from the roof of the Albert Warehouses into the Salthouse Dock, 85 years ago. A variety of vessels, including deep-sea sailing ships, are berthed for cargo loading. The transoceanic ships which sailed from the Salthouse in the 1850's included those to Australia of the famous Black Ball line. Several fine examples of victorian transit sheds for goods storage may be seen on the western and easterns sides of the dock.

the early wooden craft to the modern vessels built in the Cammell Laird Docks in Birkenhead.

Art and the Sea: Her Royal Highness, Princess Margaret, opened the gallery in 1988. Alongside seven magnificent sailing ship figureheads this exhibition houses a splendid collection of historical seascapes and ship paintings. Temporary exhibitions are also encouraged and staged whenever possible. As part of its international fame, Liverpool attracted ships, artists and carvers on a grand scale. It was also the custom particularly before the era of photography for ship owners to request that their captains have an artist paint a picture of their ship – be it sail or steam powered – whilst it was being unloaded.

In the Safe Passage Gallery the hazards confronted by those vessels sailing in the River Mersey Estuary and beyond into Liverpool Bay are examined. The charting of the many shipwrecks and their watery graves in these localities are highlighted. The role of the first life boat station, at nearby Formby in 1771, and the installation of radar in Liverpool – the first port in the world to operate it – are some of the remarkable features that come to light in this exhibition.

Liverpool the World Port, 1990: This portrays the altered character of the town with its distinguished public buildings, commercial centre, residential districts, public parks and voluminous warehouses to attract entrepreneurs. The base for this was the wealth of talent, unrivalled by any port, that was attracted to Liverpool in the nineteenth century.

To supplement the exhibitions in the galleries in the Main Building there have been a series of lectures and courses.

In 1992 these included Dock Engineers and Dock Engineering, Liverpool and West Africa, Sea Music and the Jason Project. In the latter two British youngsters, Jennifer Sacre and Tom West were contemporaries of the final 19 Argonauts – named after the companions of the Greek adventurer, Jason – selected from a competition in Britain and North America. Live broadcasts of the Jason expedition were beamed to the Merseyside Maritime Museum lecture theatre from the coverage of the underwater expedition led by American scientist Dr. Robert Ballard to the Sea of Cortez, Mexico. Audiences in Liverpool were thus able to enjoy at first hand the experience of scientific exploration underwater. For two weeks, live pictures of scientists studying hydrothermal vents and grey whales were relayed onto three giant TV screens at the Merseyside Maritime Museum.

During the 1990s a series of special exhibitions and events were organised by the Museum during the summer months when the numbers of sightseers greatly increased.

Suggested outdoor trail activities are also available from the Education Services. Sightseers, young and old, with school groups or not, will discover that a short walk outside the Maritime Museum main building will bring

Duke's Dock, c 1904
This unusual dock which lies immediately south of the Albert Dock, was built with private means to promote Liverpool's inland trade. For bulk cargoes, travelling landwards from the seaport there was provision, as shown for space, for barges and flats. The flats were sailing barges built with a huge rudder to help the carriage of maximum loads of cargoes such as cotton, grain and timber.

The Sailor's home, Liverpool, c 1905
Prince Albert laid the foundation stone for this mariners' sanctuary, 31 July 1846.
Situated in Canning Place, the well-regulated 'Home' helped visiting sailors to
escape from the 'landsharks' of the seaport. nevertheless, the temptations outside its
doors were infamous and are reflected in the 'Maggie May' sea shanty: "Oh, the first
time I saw Maggie, she took my breath away, She was cruising up and down in
Canning Place ... "

them to several fascinating examples of dock-based architecture and artifacts. These have been preserved thanks to the combined efforts of the M.D.C, the Maritime Museum and the Albert Dock Company. This was not achieved without exceptional commitment by all parties and a considerable investment. The Dock and its buildings' renovation was estimated at some £50 million.

Having been left open to the River Mersey after the Dock closed in 1971, the Albert Dock and its linked docks – the Canning Half-Tide, the Canning, the Salthouse and the Dukes Dock all silted up to a general depth of twelve feet. In 1973 the entire South Docks system had had to be abandoned because a collision at the Brunswick river entrance prevented the dock gates from closing. This made the whole system tidal. When these docks had to be pumped clear of tidal silt it was an additional expensive operation which added to the cost of making building structures sound.

The M.D.C. provided £20 million and the London-based Arrowcraft Group – which operated through its Liverpool-based subsidiary Albert Dock Co. Ltd. – provided some £50 million. By 1992 the total restoration costs were an estimated £100 million.

Despite such escalating costs and in the face of some initial scepticism and cynicism the public and private sectors combined to preserve and develop what was destined to become a unique national asset. The M.D.C. fortunately had grasped the opportunity to broaden its original conservation plans at the Albert Dock Precinct. This ensured that in the Maritime Park, which incorporates the Canning Pierhead where the Pilotage Buildings are sited, important examples of the architectural styles of two of the major Victorian Liverpool dock engineers were preserved.

These men were firstly Jesse Hartley, dock engineer 1824-60, who had corresponded with Philip Hardwick on many technical points about the construction of the Albert Dock. Hardwick had designed St. Katherine's Dock in London and the Albert Dock was based on this 'enclosed' design. Next, there was George Fosbery Lyster, Hartley's successor from 1861- 1897.

A short walk along the Hartley Quay, which is outside the Maritime Museum's main entrance, will bring the visitor to striking examples of the work of Hartley, Hardwick and Lyster and these are described below. Also included is a brief description of some of the interesting features that a short walk in the Maritime Park will allow the visitor to discover.

The H.M.S Conway anchor lies immediately outside the main Maritime Museum entrance. The Conway had been constructed in 1839 as a 92-gun wooden battleship and was converted in 1876 into a boys' school, or training ship. She was anchored in the River Mersey for many years before being moved to North Wales where she was unfortunately wrecked in the Menai Straits, near Anglesey in 1953.

Wapping Dock, c 1906
The function of Wapping Dock as a linkage passage within the southern docks is illustrated in this postcard. Though many sailing ships have claimed a quayside berth alongside the storage transit sheds the dock passages are relatively clear. This branch style of narrow docks, affording lengthy quay spaces on both sides was part of Jesse Hartley's intention to increase internal communication within Liverpool's south docks. Ships like those shown could off-load in one dock and move on to another without having to return to the river to do so.

Departure of Liner and Ferryboat, c 1912
This postcard vividly shows the abundance of goods that had to be transported by ferry boat across the River Mersey before the Mersey Tunnels were constucted. The floating Landing Stage has a variety of manual and horse-drawn carts to help in the movement of the goods. In the background an ocean-going liner capable of accommodating thousands of passengers is berthed at the Landing Stage.

Restoration of the Albert Dock
After the Albert Dock's closure in 1972 it became silted up by the River Mersey. The interior of the Dock is seen above as the final stage of the restoration process is nearly complete, the training ship, 'Royalist', a Sea Cadet Vessel is seen in the foreground.

Canning Half-Tide Dock, 1984
Crowds gather to view and to board, whenever possible, some of the smaller sailing craft moored in the Canning Half-Tide Dock, in 1984. More than twenty such vessels were to visit the Albert and Canning Docks in the 1992 Tall Ship's Festivities.

Just beyond the anchor on the Hartley Quayside
overlooking the Canning Half-Tide Dock are railway
tracks leading left to the Hartley cast-iron swing bridge.
This spans the ships' passage between the Half-Tide Dock
and the Albert Dock. Dock engineer Jesse Hartley had
designed this manually-operated bridge and it was built
in the Haigh Foundry of Wigan in 1843. Constructed in
two halves, they were operated from opposite banks. To
minimise damage to ships, the handrail folded inwards
when the bridge opened. It is the only surviving example
of its type in the South Docks where such bridges were
once widely used.

The Hartley Quayside rail tracks which run from right to
left outside the main museum entrance are reminders of
the limited construction of dock lines of railway from
1842. The lines were generally unpopular with the Dock
Trustees because of their fears that they might lose their
complete control over the docks to a rival authority.
Fortunately for the South Docks the railway promoters
were able to introduce a branch goods line from Edge
Hill – which was connected to Manchester – to
Wapping and also a goods depot opposite the Queens
Dock. In 1841 the Dock Trustees obtained an Act of
Parliament to lay tramroads or railways on the dock quays.

The development of a docks' railway network was
initially inspired by visions of accelerated dock
construction and not to promote more efficient cargo
handling. By 1851 the railway lines along the South Docks
were connected to the London and North Western

Railway Co. depot at Wapping. During the next two decades a number of branch lines were laid including that in 1866 at the Canning Dock to connect with a 10-ton crane. All the trains were horse-drawn, with a maximum of six wagons proceeding at no more than walking pace and with five-minute intervals between each train. Steam locomotives were not allowed on the dock lines until 1872. Locomotive-drawn trains finally began, in 1866, to run along the line of the South Docks. Not until 1895 was the use of locomotives in the docks permitted under a bye-law. New bye-laws directed that any locomotive should not exceed 3 mph and a man carrying a red flag should walk in front at a distance of no more than 15 feet. Even as late as 1885 the great numbers of horse-drawn carts severely limited the use of rail transport at the docks. The pumphouse and Dock Traffic Office – now Granada TV studios – to the left of the Main Museum building will be described below.

The special Museum 'trail' after the Hartley swing bridge leads to the Piermaster's House, the Policeman's Office, Mermaid House and the Dock Gatemen's Huts.

The Piermaster's House: The house was formally re-opened, July 27th 1984, by Ben Shaw, Chairman of the Merseyside County Council. Together with the Cooperage and Mermaid House, the Piermaster's House was saved from dereliction by the Merseyside County Council. This was only possible after the buildings, including their foundations were stripped and practically rebuilt. Philip Hardwick had originally designed the house and it was

Tall Ships by night, Vittoria Dock, 1992
Ships lanterns glitter 'like so many glow-worms in a grove', in Birkenhead. Unlike the Tall ships of the Victorian times the ships in the Vittoria dock in 1992 had their masts and spars illuminated by electric power. The effect of this however, was to provide an equally stunning effect at night.

Juan Sebastian de Elcano, Spain, 1992
This magnificent four-masted vessel is seen with sails unfurled in the centre of Liverpool's River Mersey. The Port of Liverpool Buildings and Albert Dock warehouses from part of the splendid backdrop on the waterfront. The vessel is now used to train officers for the Spanish Navy.

Alexander Von Humboldt, Germany, 1992
This striking vessel with its green sails and hull is seen down river from Liverpool's historic waterfront. She became the pride of the Sail Training Association of Germany and took civilian youngsters on training voyages.

The Sedov, CIS, the world's largest sailing ship, 1922
The largest sailing ship in the world, The Sedov, sails majestically out of the River Mersey. Thousands of admirers enjoy some of Liverpool's most notable landmarks such as, St Nicholas Church, the Liver building, the Cunard and the Port of Liverpool Buildings, and the Cathedral of St James.

completed in 1852 near the Canning river entrance. Three other houses – including one for the Superintendent of the Albert Dock Warehouses – were lost in the Second World War, 1939-45. The quality of the post-war restoration work owed much to the good fortune in locating several men and women who had lived during their childhood at or near the Piermaster's House.

Piermaster James Spence had lived there from about 1900 to 1907. Other Piermasters are known to have followed him. Between 1919 and 1926, Gilbert Jameson had lived there and his son and daughter – Mr. W. Jameson and Mrs M. Cleaton – helped in the restoration of this house which held fond memories of life in their former family home. A Dockmaster, W. H. Wilcox had lived at No. 8 'round the corner'. His daughter, Mrs E. M. Parry, added her recollections about the Albert Pierhead where she had grown up. Their precise and unique memories helped in the restoration of many of the original features and today they possess an air of dramatic authenticity. The interior is almost exactly as it was in the two decades, from 1900 to 1920, except for the modern heating in the ceiling and a new back staircase, which permits access for today's visitors.

A contemporary 'Piermaster's Wife' is often on hand to act as an interpreter in the house and demonstrates a variety of former household chores. The visitor may now move through the house. Firstly, in the kitchen which was the main living room, cooking was carried out on a coal- fired range. The big fitted cupboard was used for food storage, for crockery and for table linen. All meals were to be eaten here.

Moving into the back-kitchen the sightseer will be informed that herein was the only supply of water in the home. Food was prepared, 'washing-up', and the washing of clothes and their ironing was undertaken in this room. Next to the fireplace is a copper utensil for boiling water on any 'washday'. This was also the time for using the dolly tub, dolly peg, and cast-iron mangle there.

On Sundays and other occasions when special visitors might arrive they were shown into the parlour. This was filled with the best furniture and any souvenirs – including the turtle shell at the fireplace – that the Piermaster may have brought back from his days at sea.

In contrast the bedrooms are sparsely furnished. Cast-iron and brass beds with horse-hair mattresses seem to 'fill' the bedrooms. Fires would be lit only in times of illness and the wash stands were used with cold water for a daily wash.

The Piermaster's Office is at the side of the Piermaster's House and was built to Jesse Hartley's design in the 1840's. As was customary with many offices in Liverpool that had shipping connections there was an 'outer office'. Though this was usually for the clerks in this building it was for the senior gateman and all callers were expected to report to him. The inner office was for the Piermaster himself.

A Line of Tall Ships in the Vittoria Dock
Some of the densely packed crowds of admirers of the Tall Ships are seen here, in 1984. The sightseers thronging the quayside of the Vittoria Dock are seeking the closest possible view of the ships.

Vittoria Docks and the Tall Ships, 1984
Some of the largest of the Tall Ships were moored at the long quays of Birkenhead's Vittoria Dock. The vessels rested majestically at the end of another day in which immense crowds had visited these ships.

M. T. Brocklebank This motorised tug formerly belonged to the Alexandra Towing Co Ltd.

The Canning Half-Tide Dock, 1984
These splendid vessels – including the Spirit of Merseyside in the foreground and the Wincham – are seen in the Canning Half-Tide Dock. Beyond are the Pilotage Buildings which overlook the River Mersey. In 1993 the buildings housed the Museum of Liverpool Life

The Piermasters formed one strand of a hierarchy – which included Dockmasters and Gatemen – that had gradually evolved to supervise everyday work at the docks in the nineteenth century. Many of those chosen as Dockmasters had been ships' pilots or master mariners. In their new role they were expected to be at the Pier Heads to oversee the safe and efficient passage of vessels through their docks. Like the Piermasters they had to be present at any day or night 'tide times' when ships or smaller craft sought berths to 'tie up' at.

Dockmasters also supervised the dock gatemen and dock watchmen, made sure that quaysides were clean and that they recorded the main events that occurred within their docks each day. Being on call at all times they were provided with the use of a dockside, purpose-built house that was free of rent and taxes.

Their subordinates, the Piermasters had their duties principally restricted to the taking of vessels in and out of the docks. They came to the fore when Liverpool's docks became so crowded that the Dockmasters were unable to deal with every detail within their docks. The Piermasters would then direct and assist as each vessel's ropes were 'layed on', slackened or 'cast off' at the ships hauling into or out of the dock basins. They further ensured that no damage occurred to the piers, mooring posts, chains or 'mushrooms'.

In time their duties were strictly set out in conditions of service which also carried the threat of instant dismissal for a serious breach of them. The practical knowledge and experience of such men was regarded as essential and for this reason they had usually won promotion from the ranks of the Head Gatemen.

The latter had in turn been chosen from the ordinary gatemen. Promotion to the much sought after post of Piermaster usually carried a annual salary, a uniform and a house – or housing allowance – such as the one on the Albert Pierhead. Gatemen's duties will be outlined below.

The Cooperage: The Cooperage, which is situated behind the Piermaster's Office was built as a workshop about 1848. Wooden barrels that were damaged when landed at the Albert Dock were repaired there. When metal casks finally replaced the barrels the Cooperage became used as a hydraulic engineers' workshop and as a store. Today, with its restoration to its original usage a time-served cooper is a popular attraction here on most days, when he demonstrates his rare skills.

Mermaid House: Emerging from either the Piermaster's House or the Piermaster's Office a short walk to the right, towards the Tate Gallery, will bring the visitor past the Dock Policeman's Office and face to face with Mermaid House which is set back to the right of the Tate Gallery. The importance of the Dock Policemen has been outlined in a chapter above. The Tate Gallery will be described below.

Mermaid House is a small unit in those buildings
described above that were rescued from dereliction by the
Merseyside County Council. The house, with its small
upstairs private library, is the headquarters of the
volunteer group known as the Friends of Merseyside
Maritime Museum.

Its members are actively involved in supporting the
Merseyside Maritime Museum and offer help in several
ways including its 'Slide and Guide Service'. It organises
social events and has an annual lecture programme. It also
publishes its own journal, The Mermaid. Its other
voluntary activities include boat maintenance of all types
of craft. Particular favourites include the routine
maintenance of the Museum's Pilot Cutter, the Edmund
Gardner, and other vessels such as the De Wadden, the
Wincham and the Brocklebank. The Gardner and
Brocklebank are two sea-going vessels and are principally
the responsibility of the Wincham Preservation Society
which promotes the Museum and the Friend's. The latter
have been particularly keen to promote the facilities for
young children in the Maritime Museum Park and their
development of the Playboat facilities is mentioned below.

Dock Gatemen's Shelters: On leaving the Mermaid House
forecourt and passing the Dock Policeman's Office and
the Piermaster's House to the left, a short walk will lead to
the first of the Dock Gatemen's Shelters, or octagonal
stone 'huts' on the Albert Pierhead. This was the
Gatekeeper's Hut for the Albert Dock. The Gatekeepers
and Gatemen were supervised by the Piermaster. The

manual tasks of the former – employed by the Dock Trustees – included the operation of the dock gates and the dock bridge mechanisms. They also had to keep watch at night over the docks and their moored vessels. These men, who like the Piermaster wore a special uniform, had usually been chosen by the Trustees, and later the Mersey Docks and Harbour Board, for their experience at sea. As former seamen they were expected to be familiar with the handling of ships in or around the docks. They were also liable to be fined for any serious negligence in the carrying out of their duties.

The stone-walled huts were built to protect them from inclement winter weather and from the glare of the sun in the summer. The polygonal shape of the shelters permitted observation through a full circle. With the Dockmaster often on duty for 24 hours a day he could use their chamber floors for some rest after times of great activity at the docks. He was also able to see what was happening at any point if he was suddenly roused from his rest period.

The dock gates, at the entrance to Canning Half-Tide Dock Basin supervised by the Gatekeepers, were operated by hand and opened two hours before high tide and closed two hours after. To cope with growing numbers of sightseers who use this route over the 'new' footbridge at the entrance to the Canning Dock Half-Tide Basin an even wider footbridge was constructed in 1993.

The Pilotage Building. Within a short walking distance of

the stone Dock Gatemen's Shelters on the Canning
Pierhead is the Pilotage Building. This tall, red brick
building on the river front was built in 1883. It reflected
the modest character of the purpose-built dockside homes
of this era. Elements of the Queen Anne style of
architecture are evident in the building which was
designed by G. F. Lyster. This style was probably adopted
since a minimum of expense was exercised in any
essentially functional buildings at the docks. The Pilotage
Service was composed of highly experienced Master
Mariners whose duty it was to guide larger vessels
through the dangerous channels of both Liverpool Bay
and the Mersey Estuary. The Pilotage Building was a
home for those officers of the Service between 1883 and
1979. After this period it became the responsibility of the
Merseyside Maritime Museum. From 1980 Museum
displays were housed here. The former Liverpool Salvage
Company Shed close to the Pilotage Building was used as
a Museum Boat Hall.

To the front of the Pilotage Building which faces the river,
were offices on two floors and there was a flat above for
the caretaker. At the rear of the building there are two
wings separated by a courtyard. This was roofed over in
1979. The wings had provided store rooms, workshops
and a billiard room for those pilots waiting for their
vessels. There was also storage space for carts and small
boats.

A platform was erected on the roof, in 1907, to facilitate
signalling by semaphore to vessels in the river. That

method eventually gave way to the electric telegraph and then two-way radio systems.

This was a great change since the first days of the Liverpool Pilotage Act of 1776 when a rather basic system for piloting ships into and out of the port of Liverpool had been implemented. Pilot vessels, when instructed, cruised to a station at sea to intercept and 'lead', or pilot, those ships entering the Liverpool Pilotage District.

The earliest pilot vessels had been cutters and sloops which were superseded in the nineteenth century by schooners and – in 1896 – by steam vessels. In the 1950's diesel electric ships, such as the Edmund Gardner in the Canning Graving Docks, took over the duty. The provision of pilots to wait 'on station', near the mouth of the River Mersey, was finally withdrawn in 1982.

Pilots are now taken to and from ships by small launches that sail directly from Liverpool or Point Lynas in Anglesey, North Wales.

On May 3rd 1993, the Lord Mayor of Liverpool, Rosemary Cooper, officially opened the Museum of Liverpool Life in the Pilotage Building.

The Canning Graving Docks: Leaving the Pilotage Building by the rear or dock-facing entrance will lead the visitor to the two Canning Graving Docks. These are two dry docks which were constructed in 1795 and enlarged both in 1813 and 1842. They were principally used to repair ships. After a ship was pulled into a dock by labourers using a capstan the gates were shut and the water removed. This was originally done by sluices which were opened into the River Mersey at low tide. Later the docks were de-watered by pumps that were also brought into action if water entered the dock by seepage through the floor or through the dock gates. Those ships under repair were brought to rest on keel blocks and were held upright by timber baulks. By 1875 when the horizontal centrifugal pump was introduced it became possible to de-water a graving dock when occupied by a ship, in one hour. The Canning Graving Docks were used to repair merchant sailing ships, flatboats and dredgers. When work on these was completed the water was re-admitted, the ships were floated and later on hauled out.

Pitch Boilers: In the Graving Docks pitch was heated in boilers made by the Phoenix Foundry of Liverpool, c. 1810.

Any wooden vessels that needed to be made watertight had the joints between their planks filled with oakum and then coated with hot tar. This process was known as caulking the ship and was extremely arduous. The men often had to work on joints that were above their heads and a hot pitch or tar spill could prove fatal.

The pitch had to be heated in the boilers and then ladled into barrels. These were then lowered down the 'barrel runs' to those men waiting underneath the vessel.

The pitch boilers were basically brick-lined furnaces built

into the bases of large iron pots and their tall chimneys emitted strong smoke fumes.

The Edmund Gardner No. 2 Pilot Boat: This is in the Canning Dock which is overlooked by the Great Western Railway Goods Shed. As mentioned above the Edmund Gardner is a diesel-electric pilot boat. Launched in July 1953 it replaced the Walker J. Chambers as No. 2 Pilot Boat. The Edmund had been built in Dartmouth by Philip and Son, Ltd.

She was able to accommodate a maximum crew of 54. When on active duty these might consist of eleven officers and crew, eleven apprentices, and as many as 32 pilots.

Two motorised punts provided communication between the pilot boat and those ships either entering or leaving the port.

Good fortune favoured the vessel because in her 28 year period of Pilotage Service she undertook her duties without a major calamity. Considered especially seaworthy in heavy weather she was known to remain at her station in a storm with force eleven winds. In the course of the 1954 Dock Strike she regularly delivered newspapers and mail to those ships anchored at the Mersey Bar. She also provided assistance to injured seamen or distressed yachtsmen.

Her most fortuitous escape was probably in 1963 when she was in collision with the ore-carrier Iron Horse. The latter suffered steering gear failure in the Mersey and hit the Edmund Gardner on her port side. The ship rolled heavily and suffered damage to her bridge deck and her hull plating. She was fortunate to escape with no serious injuries and no lasting damage below her water line.

The Great Western Railway Goods Shed: This overlooks the Edmund Gardner Pilot Boat in the Canning Graving Dock. As mentioned above, in the development of rail tracks in the Liverpool Docks, steam locomotives were not permitted on the dock lines until 1872. In this year the London and North Western Railway Co. was granted permission to draw wagons in the Northern Docks between Canada Dock goods station and the timber yards north of Battery Street. In the same year the Great Western Railway rented accommodation around the Manchester Dock. This was sited behind the present Great Western Railway Goods Shed where the small museum car park at Mann Island is now. Goods were received at the shed and sent by barge across the River Mersey to a railway depot in Birkenhead. From here the goods were sent to Chester and then on to the Great Western Railway stations of the South West of England. A fire in the warehouse near the site of the present shed spurred the Great Western Railway to erect its own goods shed. The depot remained in use for storage until 1960 and was adapted in time by the museum for use as a conservation centre. It has recently been restored to its original Great Western Railway appearance.

The De Wadden Auxiliary Schooner: This three-masted

auxiliary schooner is strikingly visible in the second Canning Graving Dock outside the Pilotage Building.

Built in Holland in 1917, the De Wadden was one of the first schooners – originally powered purely by sail – to be fitted with an engine as her main source of propulsion. As the Great War, 1914-18, ended she was still active in coastal trade around Europe. In 1922, she was bought by Captain Richard Hall of Arklow, Ireland. He was a schooner owner who had served as an apprentice in some of the square-rigger sailing ships of Liverpool. Though he left the rigging and general deck arrangements unchanged he made a number of alterations – chiefly to the hold to provide crew quarters.

Between 1922 and 1961 the ship was kept busy in the Irish Sea, and was also well known on the Mersey as one of the last to be engaged there in commerce. She was especially welcome as a visitor to Garston. Here she loaded coal for Ireland and carried other cargoes such as grain, timber, china clay and iron ore. Her usual crew of six included the captain, engineer, bosun, cook, an able seaman and a boy apprentice. She was regarded as a happy ship by those who sailed in her and when asked about her they usually reported fond memories of their experiences aboard her.

After her sale, in 1961, she moved to Greenock, in Scotland. Her career in the next two decades still continued to attract interest. In the popular television series, The Onedin Line, she made regular appearances. She was also used for fishing expeditions.

Further alterations to her – such as the large saloon on the top of the after hatch with a wheelhouse abaft it – dramatically altered her appearance, perhaps to her detriment. In time she became commercially unviable. Fortunately, she was finally acquired by the Merseyside Maritime Museum.

When she returned to the Mersey, in August 1984, for the first time in twenty-three years it proved both an emotional and an historic occasion. The last trading schooner to sail on the river had returned in the same year as the Tall Ships Festivities. The efforts to fully restore her have been magnificent. The saloon has been restored to its original appearance. A damaging accumulation of rust has been removed and new masts have been acquired for her.

Quayside Collections: Around the Canning Graving Dock quaysides – and on the quayside between the Graving Dock and the Half- Tide Dock in particular – is an interesting collection of small boats and 'heavy metal' nautical objects.

The boats include a long wooden boat or 'whaler'. The heavy metal collection includes ships' guns, anchors, chains, propellors and quayside capstans. The pulling of vessels into the Graving Dock was done by dockers using capstans. The dock labourers had to push against wooden poles fitted into the sockets of a capstan above its barrel. When they turned the capstan a mooring rope, or warp, wound itself around the barrel and drew the vessel in. A system of pawls and ratchets prevented the capstan slipping backwards if the men stopped pushing. A number of different shaped capstans may be seen on the quaysides.

To moor the vessel to the quayside the 'dockers' attached ropes from the ships to the bollards on the quayside. Seventeen different examples of bollards may be found by the inquisitive sightseer. The most common is the round-headed cast-iron type believed to have been designed by Jesse Hartley.

A further example of his genius is the cast-iron suspension footbridge which spans the passage between Canning Dock and Canning Half- Tide Basin. It has cast-iron upright pillars supporting iron bars made of wrought-iron, not chains or cables as in the more commonplace bridges. Hartley is believed to have constructed the bridge during the Canning Dock reconstruction of the 1860's.

A walk along the northern quayside of the Canning Half-Tide Dock towards the Canning Island may reveal the Wincham and the motor tug, Brocklebank, moored in the Half-Tide Dock. These are the two handsome seagoing vessels which as mentioned above are the responsibility of the Wincham Preservation Society. The vessels take part in the Mersey's Annual River Festival and regularly attend other festivals to represent a successful working partnership between the Maritime Museum and the Preservation Society.

The Wincham was formerly a River Weaver packet ship. It delivered many cargoes from Northwich's chemical works to Liverpool. It is a single screw motorised ship that is powered by a 256 British Horse Power Crossley diesel engine. After transporting Imperial Chemical Industries' products from Northwich to Liverpool she was accustomed to berthing alongside larger vessels and discharging her cargoes into the holds of other ships.

The vessel was used for docking trials at the new Canning entrance on June 13th 1984. It became the first craft to enter into the Canning Dock system after nearly twenty years.

Like the Wincham, the motor tug Brocklebank also has strong links with Cheshire. The tug was built in 1965 by W. J. Yarwood and Sons of Northwich, Cheshire. Its gross tonnage is 17.5 tons and is powered by an 8-cylinder turbo charged 1200 British Horse Power, Crossley diesel engine. As a harbour tug it joined the Alexandra Towing Company fleet in 1965. Towage and other duties in the port of Liverpool and the Irish Sea included the towing of stone-laden barges from Anglesey to build the new Seaforth Dock. It also assisted many types of ships such as tankers, container ships, warships, cargo liners of the Clan Line and the Harrison Line and liners of the Cunard fleet.

A further notable point in her career came in 1984 when she attended the Royal Yacht Britannia during the Tall Ships' Festivities in that year. In 1989 she was purchased by the National Museums and Galleries on Merseyside. As one of the last classic single-screw River Mersey tugs it is a much respected seagoing vessel.

Looking across the Canning Half-Tide, past the main Maritime Museum Building, the visitor should be able to see the Pump House adjacent to the Dock Traffic Office the present day home of Granada TV News Studios.

The Pump House was built with a minimum of external features from the plans of the architect and dock engineer, George Fosbery Lyster. The Victorian outer brickwork and faintly machiolated chimney were treated no differently than the numerous other tall chimneys built in the seaport at this time. However, its brick masonry, particularly that of the pointed window of the engine-house has become rare since the demolition programme on the docks in the present century. It served until 1905 before its pumps were replaced by others elsewhere. The building was taken over by ships' chandlers – James Newton Co. Ltd. – in 1915. The modern interior of the present public house is both welcoming and cosy.

The Dock Traffic Office, today's Granada TV News Studios, date from 1848. Situated adjacent to the Pump House in the north east of the Albert Dock, its position was advantageous for dealing with the immense dock traffic of the last century. In that era numerous horse-drawn vehicles entered and left the Albert Dock site via the Salthouse Dock entrance which faced the imposing Georgian Custom House.

The Office was probably designed by Philip Hardwick who shared responsibility with Jesse Hartley for the Albert Dock warehouses, and the smaller dock buildings. The precise contribution of each of these men is uncertain. It has been suggested that after Hardwick's initial plans Hartley probably deepened the portico and strengthened the cornice between the second floors. He may also have 'built on' an upper or second floor to accommodate the principal clerk at the dock office.

When the building was first completed it consisted of a central public hall – which was open to the roof – with offices leading from it at two levels. Beneath the offices was a basement. The building still retains several ornate features including the tall chimney stacks and cast-iron classical portico. The Traffic Office now houses Granada Television News and during its daily news bulletin one of its upper floor studios may be seen to look out across the Canning Half-Tide Dock.

The Tate Gallery Liverpool:
An invaluable contribution to the regeneration of the Albert Dock was made when the Tate Gallery Liverpool was opened in the western warehouse by H.R.H. Prince Charles, in 1988. It was voted Fine Art Museum of the Year in 1989.

The name Tate had hitherto been renowned for the high quality of sugar produced at the seaport's Love Lane refinery. Unfortunately this was closed in 1981 and the Tate connection with Liverpool appeared to have come to an end. At the end of the 1980's, however, it rose to the fore again when the Trustees of the Tate Gallery London came face to face with a growing crisis over the showing of their unique collection of Modern Art. By the end of the decade they became able to display only twenty per cent of their acquisitions at any one time.

Following an intense search in several cities in the North of England they focused their attention on the striking dock architecture of Jesse Hartley's warehouses in the Albert Dock. The qualities of outer strength and permanence of the warehouses appeared to them to be reinforced by the building's inner spaciousness. From the outset they became regarded as highly desirable for conversion into new gallery space.

The conversion project was awarded to Liverpool-educated James Stirling of James Stirling, Michael Wilford and London Associates. Stirling had lived in Liverpool during his infancy as the son of a Master Mariner who had himself sailed from the South Docks. In his youth the younger Stirling was educated at Liverpool's Quarry Bank High School, as were John Lennon, Paul McCartney and George Harrison, and went on to study at the City's School of Architecture.

Whilst at the school he familiarised himself with both overseas and British Museum Schemes and locally he became appreciative of the architectural monumentality of Hartley's warehouses. Stirling's own later achievements included his work at the Clore extension to the Tate's Gallery at Millbank.

In the 1980's he was asked to examine the major problems that could hinder the conversion of a section of Hartley's Western Warehouse into new gallery space. A range of difficulties were laid before him by the Tate Conservators. He was asked, for example, to submit plans for the provision of the many services that thousands of visitors would need each year.

Displays of twentieth century works of art also demanded highly sophisticated lighting and air-conditioning systems. These became essential for works of art which would be drawn from the National Collection of Modern Art at Millbank and from exhibitions in the United Kingdom and throughout the world.

There were also inherent dangers from local air pollution and the seasonal loss of energy that any new gallery would have to face. Stirling's response was dramatic. He decided that a central core had to be built into the northern end of the West Warehouse. The core was to contain essential services – such as stairs, elevators, emergency escape stairs, toilets and the air-conditioning ducts. Beneath each ceiling for the full length of each floor, a double duct had to be inserted to contain the vital air-conditioning and lighting systems.

The air-conditioning had to be of a high enough standard to arrest any pollution from the heavy sulphur dioxide content in the air. The lighting requirements were met by the Phillips' Company of Holland. The latter was achieved by the provision of sophisticated reflectors which served to bounce light to and fro behind the fluorescent tubes. Additional effects for the works of art were achieved by the use of spotlights and up-lighters.

Since the warehouse for the Gallery was sited alongside the River Mersey a chill factor – particularly in the winter months – was a further major problem that had to be solved. The energy loss was exacerbated by the brick wall and the regular opening of the entrance doors to the Gallery. To reduce heat loss an internal wall, capable of allowing a six inch width of insulation by fibreglass was built. Beneath the roof, to help reduce heat escape through the ceiling, a four and one half inch cork insulation barrier was installed. The process was completed by the triple glazing of the windows – some still permitting daylight to enter and allowing the visitor memorable views across the River Mersey.

The Gallery was expertly finished with internal fittings and a layout that stimulated a sense of ease for the display of contemporary works of art. The timber wall panelling, the polished wooden upper floors of English Beech and the use of screening for dividing the Gallery into sections served to produce an interior softness that contrasted splendidly with Jesse Hartley's exterior distinctive fortress style.

Visitors may easily identify the Gallery and its quayside by the bright external scheme of blue with orange bars. It is comprised of six floors in total and includes a mezzanine with a book shop and a coffee shop. Sited just beyond the Hartley Bridge and the Piermaster's House it is strikingly popular with visitors. Admission is free to the main collections but for special exhibitions there is a charge.

The location of the Tate Gallery's Exhibition, Displays and Facilities: The gallery's exhibitions, displays and facilities have been planned by experts and the friendly, relaxed atmosphere is most reassuring for visitors.

Basement: Here there are toilets for the public, including those for the disabled, a 'baby change' room, cloakroom, storage areas and principal plant room.

Mezzanine and Ground Floor: On the ground floor most of the mezzanine has been removed to provide a spacious entrance. Helpful staff are also at hand at the information desk at the entrance. There is a coffee shop, in the mezzanine, with book shop and administration offices near at hand. The ground floor has three double height galleries for displays from the Tate Gallery's primary collections and occasional exhibitions. Work by Joseph Beuys and David Hockney were established as main exhibitions here.

First Floor: This is regarded as the principal temporary exhibition space for both the contemporary and the modern art exhibitions. New Realities: Art in Post War Europe, 1945-1968, has been a principal exhibition to date. Another gallery and interpretation rooms will be completed in Phase 2 of the Tate's development.

Second Floor: This floor is to be devoted to displays in depth from the Tate Gallery's collections. In Phase 2 there will also be extended education facilities on this floor.

Third Floor: Principally used for storage facilities at present.

Fourth Floor: All of this floor will be completed in Phase 2. Part of it, with a modified roof will be used for performances, contemporary dance, lectures and films. The Gallery will be devoted to international contemporary exhibitions or 'installations' and there will be a suite of studios for artistes-in-residence and restaurant facilities. The building is fully accessible to the disabled.

The cost of the entire warehouse conversion for Tate Gallery Liverpool had been estimated in 1984 at £9.5m. For Phase 1, £4.5m was offered by the Merseyside Development Corporation and £0.5m by the Office of Arts and Libraries. A further £2.0m was raised by corporate and individual patrons and their names are displayed on the ground floor. Refurbishment began in October 1985 and was completed by mid-1986, and fitting out was completed in 1988. After the completion of Phase 2, which will involve further development on the second floor and the conversion of the whole of the fourth floor, Tate Gallery Liverpool will then be able to offer 2,700 square metres of gallery space. This will then be equivalent to the area which is devoted to Modern Art in the Tate in London. The cost of the Phase 2 conversion is currently estimated at a further £2.5 million.

The Liverpool Tate, meanwhile, continues to grow in popularity and like the Merseyside Maritime Museum, it has its own special group of supporters. The Tate Gallery Supporters were formed in 1989 to raise funds to promote the Gallery throughout the North of England. Such is their success that they have been able to offer a wide range of benefits to their members. These benefits include invitations to private views, special Supporters events, visits, talks and free admission to paying exhibitions both at Tate Gallery Liverpool and Tate Gallery London. Such members play a vital role in contributing to the continuing growth and development of the Gallery.

Audience development is indeed regarded as central to the Gallery's key aims and the Tate's programme is now recognised as being among the most innovative in the country. Workshops, talks, study days, 'open studios' and outreach projects have all been designed to meet the needs of families and interested individuals, educational and community organisations and special needs groups.

Tate Gallery Liverpool workshops are also worthy of mention for they incorporate a wide variety of activities and are run by individuals with a broad range of skills. Gallery staff, visual artists, historians, poets, performers and musicians have taken on the running of workshops. There are in-service sessions for teachers and resources – including information packs and slide-packs – which are available for schools. Details of current programmes may be obtained by reference to the Gallery's Newsletter and Viewpoints leaflets. Further information may also be obtained from the Education Department, Tate Gallery Liverpool.

Through its presentation and interpretation of the National Collection of Modern Art, the Tate Gallery Liverpool continues to be refreshingly innovative and challenging in ways that have increased the understanding and enjoyment for all its visitors. With more than 600,000 visitors annually, the Gallery has proved an outstanding attraction and a vital invigorating force in the Albert Dock success story.

Such success enabled the Albert Dock to become recognised as a fitting centre for a series of events with world-wide, maritime significance. The Tall Ships's visits, 1984 and 1992 – together with the Battle of the Atlantic Commemoration, between May 26th and 31st, 1993 – moved the eyes of the world to focus on Merseyside.

During each of these occasions the Albert Dock and its linkage docks were especially popular for those sightseers seeking a closer inspection of the vessels moored therein. Indeed several other historic docks in Liverpool, Bootle and Wirral also proved to be ideal for the viewing of those ships that had been selected for public inspections.

The role of the River Mersey and its docks had been crucial in the Battle of the Atlantic, 1939-43. The Battle had been the most prolonged campaign of the Second World War. The first encounter with the enemy took place within twelve hours of war being declared – the last occured five years, eight months and four days later.

Liverpool became Britain's principal convoy port during the war-time years. The seaport helped to preserve a lifeline, especially with the USA and Canada, which was essential to Britain's survival and the ultimate victory of the Allied Powers.

An average of three to four convoys arrived each week in the River Mersey – more that one thousand in all during the War. From 1941, the year of the May Bombing Blitz of Liverpool, the headquarters of the Western Approaches Command – the nerve centre for the planning and organisation of the battle – was centred in the seaport. The Albert Dock itself was used for refitting warships and submarines.

Warships and merchant ships in large numbers were also built and repaired in other Mersey docks. Thousands of local people were directly involved in the Battle of the Atlantic acting either as Royal Naval or Merchant Navy personnel, dock workers, port service workers or as shipbuilders.

It was thus appropriate that the Commemoration of the 50th anniversary took place on the River Mersey. HMS Cornwall and HMS Ark Royal were to be moored in the River near the Albert Dock. The Albert and Canning Docks also became a major base for special activities during the commemoration. Some of the smaller naval vessels were also berthed at the Albert and Canning Docks and opened for public visits.

During the commemoration period, Her Royal Highness, the Queen, visited the Albert Dock and took the opportunity to mingle with some of the veterans of the Battle of the Atlantic who assembled there. She also made a special visit to the Merseyside Maritime Museum, 28th May 1993, to mark the completion of its main refurbishment programme.

Her presence helped to continue the Royal association so inextricably linked with the Albert Dock. This was a further remarkable chapter in what must surely be one of the outstanding rejuvenation stories of the twentieth century and one that assisted Liverpool in its re-establishment as a popular international meeting place. An estimated six million visitors annually travel to the Albert Dock.

The Queen later thanked the people of Merseyside for their 'special welcome' during the Battle of the Atlantic Commemoration period. She particularly praised the warmth of the greetings she had received on both sides of the River Mersey. This glowing tribute was set out in a letter sent to Liverpool's newly elected Mayor, in 1993, Michael Black. Such frankness perhaps compared to Prince Albert's remark – –"I have heard of the greatness of Liverpool but the reality far surpasses the expectation" – made more than one hundred and forty years before when the Albert Dock was named in his honour.

Appendix

The Head Constable's report on the calamitous fire in Crompton Street and neighbourhood. Vol. 2. Watch Committee Records. 28. IX 1842.

" ... a few minutes before 3 o'clock on Friday morning September 23rd, 1842, a fire was discovered in one of the many temporary wooden buildings in Crompton Street, and although the alarm was instantly given several of them were in flames before the arrival of the engines; four of these quickly got into play, one supplied from an engine placed at the dock and two others from the water carts, but as the space occupied by the flames extended from Crompton Street to the warehouses north side of Formby Street, there was no possibility of approaching the back of the warehouse, the windows of 3 of which were in five minutes, on fire; ...

" ... For a time we flattered ourselves that we should succeed but the wind increasing in the vicinity of the fire to almost a hurricane, we found it impossible to reach the catheads although we used four of the tallest ladders. The water as it issued from the nozzle of the branches was scattered about in spray. Knowing the nature of the place I immediately sent a message on horseback to his worship ... saying that in my opinion every warehouse in the vicinity would be consumed.

" ... Mr. McFadzean opened the sewer, through which passed the overflow from the canal and gave an abundant supply to No/8 and No/2 ...

" ... ultimately, however, a cathead on the southside of the
street caught fire, at which an immense flame rushed across as
if from a gigantic blowpipe, igniting every door and window
opposite. Still we had hopes that two warehouses at the top
and two at the bottom could be saved, but while in the act of
getting the hose up a staircase, part of a wall fell and crushed to
death Fireman Samuel Hodgson ... cool fearless and energetic.
To extricate the other branchmen enclosed within the falling
walls was the first duty, and their safety was happily effected
but with the loss of hose, branches and ladders. They had
hardly rushed across the fallen ruins when down came
warehouse after warehouse in such rapid succession that in a
few minutes all Formby Street was a crater of fire. In the
meantime two engines had been withdrawn, to what was
considered a safe distance, but such was the insubstantial
nature of all the buildings, that one untouched by the fire was
dragged down by the others, and its fall crushed two engines,
wounded several persons, and among others, Mr.
Superintendent Riding.

"One double warehouse called a fire-proof one was still
standing. The doors and windows were, however, composed
of wood and the cathead also wood having caught fire ... the
flames then threatened the new warehouses and timber yards
opposite, there now being a good supply of water from the
dock, all these were saved ... but Mr. Poole's 2 cotton sheds in
Great Howard Street were totally consumed.

" ... Attention was now directed to Neptune Street ...
especially two cotton sheds and when I perceived the walls
tumbling down in a way I never witnessed before I begged of
them to let the men roll out the balls ... and not delay to cart
them. At this moment a wall fell through the upper end of the
roof of the rice shed covering four of the men employed in
getting out the rice ... one was extracted but little injured, one
badly hurt and 2 died after being taken to hospital. The walls
opposite the cotton sheds still stood, and 2 engines being in full

play had mastered the flames opposite when the wall fell, knocking down 4 men employed in getting out the cotton ... one was killed on the spot, one was rescued, and two could not be quickly extricated ... the 2 firemen had dropped their branches, the hose was covered with cotton bags, and all I could do, could not persuade any one to come to their assistance. The firemen, however, quickly returned, and while in the act of getting the hose ready to cool the place round the men Mr. Superintendent Quick rushed in and dragged us from under a descending pile of cotton ... In a moment the whole was in flames and the unfortunate men were literally burned alive. The next object was the protection of the borough gaol; men were employed on the roof in throwing water, ... about half past nine 'o'clock the fire had reached its limits but the engines continued in full play all that day and night. Mr. Hewitt and myself being exhausted and almost blinded by the heat ... retired ... The loss is immense, several sheds, a cooperage and a wheelright's yard in Crompton Street were consumed; in Great Howard Street two cotton sheds; in Formby Street eleven warehouses, and in Neptune Street 2 cotton sheds, a cooperage and 2 rice sheds partially injured ... "

That such a calamitous fire began in one of the main temporary buildings in Crompton Street supports the report of Liverpool's building surveyor, William Rishton, June 28th 1859, that insufficient powers existed both to prevent the carrying on of dangerous businesses in unsuitable warehouses and to regulate the storage of combustible articles of merchandise in them before 1843.

As a direct result of such fires, as that above, the Liverpool Fire Prevention Bills, of 1843 and 1844, were passed. Merchants and brokers alike induced the Liverpool Corporation to apply to Parliament for the two statutes. As a consequence, dangerous warehouses were taken down, no more were erected for the carrying on of dangerous trades and all new property required increased space. This was apparent in 1846, when the Albert Dock was opened.

The calamitous fire described above was one in a sequence that helped stir the municipal conscience of Liverpool. Such disasters brought widespread hardship in the seaport either in the form of personal injury, ruined businesses or unemployment. Further consequences were often those heavy losses suffered by the cotton textile industry and the damage to ships that were moored alongside the dockside warehouses.

For many decades huge multi-storeyed warehouses had been built with storage departments of enormous cubic space. Their vast floors were left undivided by effective walls. Partitionings such as there was generally proved useless as fire stops because they were wantonly perforated by doors, hoists, shafts and windows. When the Goree warehouses had been razed to the ground by fire, in 1802, the quantities of grain, sugar, coffee and cotton – valued then at £323,000 – smouldered in the ruins for over three months.

The 1842 Crompton Street and district fire was reported by the Liverpool Courier in the following terms:

"The actual origin of the fire is as usual, enveloped in mystery and uncertainty but it may be imagined from the following description of the Liverpool warehousing system.

That destructive fires should occur amongst the warehouses of Liverpool is the inevitable want of plan in their formation and judgement in their location, with the consequent absence of system and responsibility in their management. Created by individuals without regard to general interests, the warehouses scattered throughout the town are frequently in close proximity to immediate sources of ignition, such as smithies, cooperages, mills, steam-engines, etc. and to these dangers, to which they are exposed from external causes, are added those from dram-shops, ships' chandlery stores and other hazardous trades which not infrequently occupy parts of warehouses filled with merchandise of immense value ....

Each warehouse being separate private property is liable to have as many tenants as rooms, or parcels of goods stored ... and to be stored by many different sets of porters ... open to the thief and the incendiary ... free from general superintendence ... exposed to danger of fire within and without, according to the doctrine of chances ... "

In something of a panic, the insurance companies raised their rates sometimes as high as over 400 per cent. They promised to reconsider these if the standard of warehousing improved, when a more dependable and more forceful water supply for fighting fires became available and when the goods within them were stored with more correct classifications, instead of being haphazardly jumbled at the whim of the warehouse owners.

A number of insurance companies also formed the Fire Salvage Association of Liverpool and from this they created the Liverpool Salvage Brigade. Included in this uniformed corps' responsibilities was the inspection of the seaport's warehouses and the issuing of their own special certificates of approval. They awarded their first certificate to the owners of Harbords Warehouses, New Quay, 2nd May 1844.

The Association had their offices and salvage equipment sited in Temple Street, close to the Central Fire Station, in readiness to act immediately upon any information they received about a fire brigade 'turn out'. This single-minded determination of these salvage operators to protect insured property left no-one in doubt.

The men of the new Salvage Brigade wore a distinctive uniform, which included small round flat-topped black leather hats inscribed with the golden letters 'Salvage'. Under their bold leader, Lieutenant Maxwell, Inspector of Salvage, they presented a new force in the projected campaign against arsonists and looters. They were soon nicknamed the 'Black Hats', being distinguished by their headwear from the silver-helmeted Fire Brigade.

After a fire they were instructed to 'sheet up' goods damaged so as to protect them from water damage. They removed any goods whenever possible and swept up and cleaned out any affected warehouses. Surplus water had to be pumped away and any machinery, etc. had to be wiped down vigorously, to prevent rust occurring. They had to make safe and guard damaged premises and remove and 'recondition' any goods worthy of such treatment. On other occasions they were regularly sent out to patrol high risk properties and make surveys to discover any defects in the storage facilities of any buildings they inspected.

When the Liverpool merchants reacted angrily to the proposed increase in insurance rates the City Council acted unequivocally and obtained the passage of a local bill through Parliament. An Act for Better Protection of Property in the Borough of Liverpool (6/7 Vic., c.x local).

Its interesting preamble read:

"Whereas fires in warehouses in the Borough of Liverpool have of late years been frequent and an alarming occurrence, and have been attended with considerable loss of life and property – and whereas it is expedient that improvements in the construction of warehouses be made ... "

The Act was uncompromising for it provided that no warehouses should be built or rebuilt "except of good materials of sufficient strength and in a substantial and workmanlike manner", and gave power to enforce the pulling down or dismantling of any building that did not comply with such provisions. No warehouse was to be larger than 4,000 'superficial' feet, nor could it be built in close proximity to other buildings. Any "Ardent spirits", such as oil, turpentine, pitch, resin, naphtha, varnish, brimstone and other hazardous stores, were to be securely stored in special warehouses. Certain trades, including those practised by ships' chandlers, colourmen, cabinet-makers and sailmakers, were not to be undertaken, except in protected buildings. The burning of oil, blubber or tar and the manufacture of turpentine, naphtha and varnish could only take place in those buildings that were segregated from others by a distance of at least seventy-five feet.

Warehouses now had to be registered in the 'town book' and as mentioned above the insurance companies, acting as one body, agreed upon a substantial discount for those that fully complied with their regulations. A safety certificate was the reward for such care and Harbords, as mentioned, was awarded the very first to be issued.

This stirring of the municipal conscience made Liverpool unique in this development of warehouse safeguards. A similar 'first' for Liverpool was that noted by the 1844 Commission of Enquiry into the State of Large Towns and Populous Districts. The seaport was again found to be exceptional in that it was the only one to have introduced a separate supply of water for the distinct purpose of protecting properties from fire. This again had been spurred on by the enormous destruction of property by fires in the City. All new warehouse property required increased interior and exterior space, too. This was apparent in 1846, when the 'showpiece' and fortress-like Albert Dock was opened.

Additional new security was added to the latter in the form of 450 Chubb and Co. patent locks of the best quality. They were regarded by their makers as probably 'the most complete lock ever made for such a purpose'. Their entire cases and mechanisms were made of copper and brass to prevent rust. Each lock had a separate and distinct key which only opened its own lock. Each under-warehouse keeper could only lock or unlock his own assigned warehouse and no other.

The Superintendent of the Docks had master keys with which he could open all 450 locks. At any time by giving any lock an extra turn with the master key, he could shut out any one of the under keys. If any attempt was made to pick or open these locks by false keys, the attempt, by means of a special inbuilt detector would prevent the 'under keys' from opening the locks. Any attempt at robbery would thereby have to be reported to the Superintendent of the Docks for only he could then restore the locks to their 'original state'.

Bibliography

Manuscript Sources

The Liverpool Watch Committee Sources
Vol.1.13.x.1838
2.1.1839
Vol.2.12.v1.1841
28.1x.1842
Vol.3.30.x11.1843
27.1v.1844
Vol.4.8.v111.1846
24.1v.1847
Vol.5.13.1x.1838
Vol.6.12.11.1853
3.v1.1854
Vol.7a.15.x1.1856
Vol.8.27.v111.1861
Vol.9.6.v1.1865
Vol.12.8.1.1872
Vol.15.2.x1.1875
Vol.17.11.11.1879

Parliamentary Papers

Report of the Select Committee on
    Drunkenness, p.p. 1834 v111.
Reports of the Inspectors of Prisons for
    the Northern and Eastern Districts.
2nd. p.p. 1837 xxx11 499
6th. p.p. 1841 (Sess.2) v1
13th. p.p. 1847-48 xxxv1 361
30th. p.p. 1865 xx111 257
Royal Commission on the Establishment
    of a Constabulary Force in England
    and Wales.
First Report p.p. 1839 x1x.
Royal Commission on the Health of
    Towns.
First Report p.p. 1844 xv11.

Books

Blackstone, G.V. 1957. *A History of the
    British Fire Service.*
Briggs, A. 1964. *Victorian Cities.*
Cockcroft, W.R. 1974. *The Liverpool Police
    Force, 1836-1902, in Victorian Lancashire*
    ed. S.P. Bell.
Dickens, C. *The Uncommercial Traveller.*
Hammond, J.L. & B. 1932. *James Stansfeld.*
Hope, E.W. 1931. *Health at the Gateway.*
Police and the Fire Brigade in Public
    Health Congress Book. 1903
Hughes, Q. 1964. *Seaport: Architecture
    and Townscape in Liverpool.*
Hugill, S. 1967. *Sailor Town.*
Kohl, J.G. 1844. *Ireland, Scotland and
    England.*
Miller, A. 1988. *Poverty Deserved?
    Relieving the Poor in Victorian Liverpool.*
Nott-Bower, J.W. 1936. *Fifty-two Years a
    Policeman.*
Ritchie-Noakes, N. 1984. *Liverpool's
    Historic Waterfront.*
Tobias, J.J. 1967. *Crime and Industrial
    Society in the Nineteenth Century.*
Waller, P.J. 1981. *Democracy and
    Sectarianism: A Political and Social
    History of Liverpool, 1868-1939.*
Webb, S. and B. 1903. *The History of
    Liquor Licensing in England.*
Winskill, P.T. and Thomas, J. 1887.
    *Temperance Movement in Liverpool and
    District 1829-1887.*
Younge, A.E. and Ashton, E.T. 1956.
    *British Social Work in the Nineteenth
    Century.*

Index